For the people of Banffshire – by the people of Banffshire

Former Coat of Arms of the County of Banff

"I LOVE BANFFSHIRE"

For the people of Banffshire
by the people of Banffshire

This Book is no. 50 of a LIMITED EDITION of 3,000 copies.

Ballindalloch Castle,
home of the Lord Lieutenant

From scenes like these, old Scotia's grandeur springs,
That makes her loved at home, revered abroad;
Princes and lords are but the breath of kings,
an honest man's the noblest work of God.

Robert Burns

"I LOVE BANFFSHIRE"

by CLARE RUSSELL

LORD LIEUTENANT OF BANFFSHIRE

Acknowledgements

My most grateful thanks first to John Fowlie, who has given me so much help and support and has always been there for me; David Findlay Clark for his excellent 'Introduction to Banffshire' and his amazing photographs; Jim McPherson for his superb 'Toast to Banff'; and the Deputy Lieutenants of Banffshire – Tricia Seligman, Jim Walker, Alan McIntosh, Peter Laing, Roger Goodyear and Scilla Gordon-Duff. Big thank-yous to my beloved family – Oliver, Guy and Victoria, Edward and MiMi, Lucy and Mike. Special thanks to Fenella for her endless patience and encouragement – without her the book might never have been printed.

Thanks to 'Team Ballindalloch' – Tim Atkinson, Kath Davies, Evelyn King, Kenny Flesh, Derek Clark, Steve Brand, David and Sue Johnstone, the late Douglas Campbell, and to all our estate employees. An enormous thank you to Amy Davenport for allowing me to use her magnificent photograph on the dust-cover of my book. Many grateful thanks also to Dawn Hargreaves, Tom Burnett-Stuart, Charles Burnett and Eleanor McIntosh. My sincere thanks also go to Nick McCann for his marvellous design, and to Martin Kempson and Kaarin Wall of Heritage House Group.

I would also like to thank for their kindness, help and support Her Majesty the Queen's Press Officer Ailsa Anderson; the Ministers of the churches photographed, the Banffshire golf courses, the 28 Banffshire distilleries, the Aberlour Highland Games Committee, Campbell & Co of Beauly, Georgina Clark, Downies of Whitehills, Robert Flett, Kate Forester, the Gordon-Duff family, Joanna Gordon, Sam Lloyd, James May, Sergeant Jappy and 'C' Company 2nd Battalion The Highlanders Army Cadet Force, Lucy McPhee, Alicia Lawson, Mary Lee-Steere, George Clark, Rachel Kennedy, Jennifer Walker, Nigel Seligman, Rebecca McCloughlin, Michael Roy, Jan Foydor, Ron Roger, Richard Hughes, Mark Williamson, and Camera Club members Frank Slowey, Alan Butterfield, Allan Adam, Alistair Paterson, Gray Garner, John Davison, John Ingle, Rae Munro, Sandy Watson, Vic Wratten, and all my friends who have kindly given me advice.

Without the fantastic photographs donated by the people of Banffshire there would be no book, so my most grateful thanks go to all the photographers, specially those who produced so many – David Findlay Clark ARPS (pp 5, 8, 9, 12, 13, 24, 37, 42, 43, 44, 45, 47, 55, 60, 61, 62, 83, 91, 113, 137, 147, 154, 155, 175); Patricia Lawson (pp 5, 46, 79, 80, 82, 87, 88, 89, 99, 107, 109, 136, 139, 140, 141, 142, 152, 161); Alan Butterfield (pp 30, 132, 133, 138, 139, 143, 148, 149, 163, 193, 194); Allan Adam (pp 10, 18, 19, 30, 49, 94, 95, 144, 149); Nick McCann (pp 2, 52, 68, 73, 75, 77, 84, 86, 88, 89, 93, 96, 110, 176, 177, 179); Rae Munro (p 121); Alistair Paterson (pp 25, 45, 49, 52, 96, 150, 165, 171); John Rennie, Cullen, Deskford & Portknockie Heritage Group (pp 10, 11, 22, 23, 26, 44, 45, 48, 151, 172, 192); Frank Slowey (pp 31, 36, 37, 45, 57, 101, 114, 115, 119, 121, 123, 146, 148) and Andrew Wells (11, 56, 63, 69, 79, 99, 107, 139, 162, 170, 196, 197). Thanks also to Toni Asher (p 112); Tim Atkinson (pp 13, 109); Colin Baxter (pp 9, 126, 127); Niall Benvie, Images from The Edge (pp 12, 54, 55, 84, 85, 104); Geoffrey Bond OBE (p 177); Buckie & District Seamen's Memorial Chapel (pp 50, 51); Charles Burnett, Ross Herald of Arms (pp 16, 17); Tom Burnett-Stuart (p 63); Canadian Pacific Railway Archives (pp 180-183); David Catto, Spey Larder (p 65); Nan Caldwell (pp 40, 41, 106, 147); Georgina Clark (p 51); Speyside Cooperage (pp 70-71); Fenella Corr (p 145); Craigellachie Distillery (p 67); Crispian Cook (p 197); Peter Wilde, Cumbria Wildlife (pp 1, 5, 108); Amy Davenport (pp 28-29); Jim Davidson (p 108); John Davison (p 45); Diageo (p 157); Ralph Diaz (pp 37, 46, 47, 58, 59, 108); David Findlay (p 37); Ian Finlayson (p 21); Langley Forbes/ John Addison (pp 32, 33); Donald Ford (pp 5, 13, 36, 38, 39, 129, 131); John Fowlie, Vice Lord Lieutenant of Banffshire (pp 18, 19, 25, 33, 165, 173, 194 and Banffshire Churches); Glasgow University Library, Special Collections (pp 168, 169); Glenfarclas Distillery (p 68); Glenfiddich Distillery (p 67); Glenlivet Distillery (pp 68, 69); Roger Goodyear, Kay Beaton & Karen Crowe, Banffshire Coast (pp 26, 27, 158); Stewart Grant (pp 56, 79, 86, 87, 141, 143, 193); Mark Hamblin (pp 5, 11, 43, 85, 98, 100, 101, 102, 103, 140); Bill Hunter (pp 21, 44, 49); Keith & Dufftown Railway (pp 122, 123); David McWilliam and Keith & District Heritage Group (pp 56, 118, 119, 171, 172); Ron King (p 141); Knock News (p 121); Stephen Lauren (p 125); Alexandra Lawson (pp 56, 107); Ted Leeming (pp 188, 189, 190, 191); Charles Lindsay from 'Lost Balls' (p 130); Sandy McCook (pp 14, 95, 99, 119, 120, 121, 134, 135); Mark McDermott (p 197); Lyn McDonald (pp 43, 47, 150, 195); Graeme McHardy (p 147); Tom McLennan (p 175); Clan Macpherson Museum (p 170); Ian Macilwain (p 37); National Trust for Scotland (p 98); 'The Northern Scot' (p 121); Orient Express (Royal Scotsman) (p 184, 185, 186, 187); John Paul (pp 121, 197); David Porter (pp 34, 35, 47); Robert Rattray (pp 78, 79, 84, 86, 87, 90); RNLI (p 48); Neil Ross (pp 88, 89); David Russell (p 156); Gene Rycroft (p 105); University of St Andrews Library of 'Special Collections' (p 124); Earl of Seafield (p 159); Sealpin Kennels (p 87); Nigel Seligman (p 167); Duncan Brown (pp 116, 117); Roy Summers (Scottish Field)(p 83); Scottish Viewpoint (p 120); Trout & Salmon magazine (p 91); VisitScotland (pp 10, 49, 66, 141); Jim Walker & Walkers Shortbread (pp 64, 65, 91, 197); Sandy Watson (p 11); Nicola Wood (p 169); and thanks to Anne Heinrich, Ann McLean, Gerald & Margaret Stewart, The Crown Estate, Paul's Hill Windfarm, CKD Galbraith, Moray Seafoods, Historic Scotland, The National Galleries of Scotland, Aberdeenshire Council, Kathy Mansfield, Jenny Stone, Val Fittall, Silvana Matheson, Michael Grant, Jack Johnston, Alex Hay, John Tasker, Andrew Taylor, George Boardman and Martin Duthie for their help. Recipe photographs (pp 53, 77, 97, 111) by Simon Walton. Grateful thanks also to our local newspapers – The Banffshire Journal, The Banffshire Herald, The Banffshire Advertiser, The Northern Scot and The Press and Journal – for permission to reproduce photographs.

I would like to acknowledge and thank where appropriate the authors of quotes, poems, sayings, songs and ballads, including the anonymous ones as well: Robert Burns (pp 2, 15, 110, 138 and Auld Lang Syne); James Copeland (p 81); James Hogg (p 68); A E Housman (p 154); John Laine (pp 87, 'Thomas & Josie's Special Treats'); Alexander Leslie (p 96); John Masefield (p 34); John Gillespie Magee (p 42); Louis Macneice (p 139); W Ferrier Mavor (p 57); Hilda Meers (p 44); Spike Milligan (p 59); Scottish Anglers' Lament (p 90); Anglers' Prayer (p 91); Mary Oliver (p 105); Sir Michael Parkinson CBE (p 128); John Rice (p 26); William Shakespeare (p 107); Dorothea Eastwood (p 103); Percy Shelley (p 11); James Russell Lowell (p 133); Stanley Bruce (p 175); Sir Walter Scott (p 191); Margaret Leith Minter (p 160); William Whiting (p 48); L N Jackson (p 94); Walter de la Mare (p 194); from 'Song of Solomon' (p 83).

I am so grateful to all those who feature in the photographs and my sincere apologies if I have identified photographs wrongly or indeed left out names of photographers. I have made every effort to contact all contributors and copyright holders of images and written content. If any omissions have occurred, I apologise and corrections and amendments will be incorporated in any subsequent editions.

I thank you all from the bottom of my heart for making this book possible.

Contents

The HISTORIC *County* *of* BANFFSHIRE

The County's location within Scotland

An INTRODUCTION *to* BANFFSHIRE

by Dr David Findlay Clark OBE, DL

Macduff Harbour

anging from the southern shore of the Moray Firth like an overfilled and lumpy Christmas stocking, the ancient County of Banffshire stretches its toe some 60 miles to the south-west. The sea laps onto or crashes into a coastline which is a mix of broad sandy beaches and high, craggy and forbidding cliffs toward its eastern boundary.

The early settlers, mainly Picts with a later scattering of Norsemen, found rich, rolling arable land inland of the raised beaches to the west and the cliff tops of the east. The major rivers, the Spey and the Deveron, drain the hinterland, much of which after the first 20 or 30 miles south from the sea, rises to 1,000, then 2,000 and, at the last point of the toe, to over 4,000 feet at the summits of Ben Macdhui and Cairngorm. Up there, where the former is the second highest mountain in the UK, there is an arctic tundra far above the tree-line which is unforgiving in the winter, if attractive to skiers, but a remote wild wilderness for the hill walkers and climbers in summer.

Bartholomew's Gazetteer of the British Isles (1887) described Banffshire as a maritime county in the NE of Scotland stretching about 56 miles between Aberdeenshire and Moray. Previously there was a small detached section within Aberdeenshire, now incorporated in the latter. The county is very narrow in proportion to its length, broadest along the north where it stretches 30 miles along the south shore of the Moray Firth. The area of the county is 640.8 square miles, population (in 1887) 62,736 – or 98 persons per square mile. The Gazetteer continues, "The greater part of the S. section (about three-fourths of the entire length) is occupied with lofty mountains, finely wooded hills, and picturesque glens.

Finishing the drills   *View of Ben Macdhui*

The N. district is beautifully diversified with low hills, fine valleys, and small tracts of rich plain. The highest mountains, Ben Macdhui (4,296ft) and Cairn Gorm (4,080ft) are grouped on the SW. border. The rivers are the Spey, with its affluent the Fiddich; the Deveron, with its affluent Isla; and the Boyne. There are quarries of slate and marble. The occupations are chiefly pastoral, but great numbers of the people are also employed in the fisheries."

While the topography has changed very little since those lines were first penned, Banffshire in the early 21st century contains a rich diversity of business and industry. Tourism is, of course, a major feature of its economy and it offers a range of activities and interesting sites (and sights) for visitors second to none in the British Isles. Few tourists will care to resist the call of the many world famous distilleries scattered about the county. Almost all will offer an interesting and informative tale about their product – not to mention a free parting dram to every visitor! Who has not heard of Glenfarclas, Glenfiddich, Glenlivet, Glendeveron, Macallan, Mortlach, Balvenie and many others? Each has its own distinctive taste and style. Each guards its secrets with assiduous intensity. Each will have you coming back for more!

Forestry and its by-products have for many years, and even in medieval times, played a large part in the economy of the county, continuing to do so with the support of enterprising companies such as Scottish Woodlands. There is a natural diversity of tree growth throughout the county which, with its mix of conifers, deciduous and decorative trees, creates an attractive rural scene. Larger plantations, mainly coniferous, can be found at all stages of maturity and there is a constant need to balance these against the effects on the wildlife and wild plant growth. All over Banffshire can be found a considerable range of wild animal and bird life.

Love's philosophy

The fountains mingle with the river
And the rivers with the ocean,
The winds of heaven mix for ever
With a sweet emotion;
Nothing in the world is single,
All things by a law divine
In one another's being mingle –
Why not I with thine?
See the mountains kiss high heaven
And the waves clasp one another;
No sister-flower would be forgiven
If it disdain'd its brother:
And the sunlight clasps the earth,
And the moonbeams kiss the sea –
What are all these kissings worth,
If thou kiss not me?

Percy Bysshe Shelley 1792–1822

11

High up there are red deer, foxes and mountain hares, pine martens and red squirrels and lower down, roe deer, badgers, more foxes, rabbits, hares, otter, mink and now, allegedly, the odd panther.

Ornithologically it is a rich hunting ground, all the way from the cliffs and seashore to the high moorlands and wild mountain tops. On the latter you may spot snow bunting, golden eagles, ptarmigan and red and black grouse. Descending, there will be hen harriers, buzzards, kestrels, sparrowhawks, curlews, lapwings, ravens, hooded crows and a wealth of the usual meadow and garden birds. On the coast, oystercatchers, terns, puffins, guillemots and every kind of gull, are just a few of the fascinating attractions to 'twitchers' and photographers.

The Eagle

He clasps the crag with hookèd hands:
Close to the sun in lonely lands
Ring'd with the azure world, he stands.

The wrinkled sea beneath him crawls;
He watches from his mountain walls,
And like a thunderbolt he falls.

Golden Eagle

Capercaillie looking for a mate

Red deer in the wild

Reindeer herd in the Cairngorms

The skilled and successful farmers of the lower Banffshire rolling fields and woodlands are amongst the most productive, acre for acre, in the world. Quite apart from supplying the barley for the distilleries, they sustain a mix of grains and vegetables from some fields and fine herds of cattle, flocks of sheep and huge piggeries in others. The Aberdeen Angus herd at Ballindalloch Castle is world famous and shares a strain with the herd of the Castle of Mey. Food processing for human consumption is carried on by one major firm and food processing for the animals themselves is a secondary product. It need hardly be added that, although EU policies have decimated the Scottish fleet generally, there is still from the ports of Macduff and Buckie a substantial output of fish and shellfish of the highest quality and diversity, with Moray Seafoods at Buckie, Downies of Whitehills, and Sutherlands of Portsoy, preparing and marketing their excellent products. Boatbuilding, and repairs and maintenance facilities for the fishing fleet are provided by Macduff and Buckie shipyards. At Aberlour, Walkers shortbread, cakes and other bakery products have found their way not only into almost every household in the land but also into several airlines, major hotels and other institutions worldwide.

It is therefore not surprising that dotted about the county are a number of first-rate restaurants and other eating places where the most fastidious of palates may be titillated. Happily, in spite of the growth of the big multiple stores, there are still independent butchers, bakers and grocers and in addition Sangs of Banff, who have produced their popular aerated drinks for many years. While mentioning names, other areas of successful local enterprise should be mentioned, such as Walkers Builders, of Banff, and in the haulage industry, A & F Grant of Ballindalloch and MacPherson of Aberlour. In the engineering field, Cheynes of Banff, and Forsyths in Buckie have excelled, providing work for many.

If your interests are more active (saving the fine food and the drams for nearer the end of the day) then Banffshire contains a range of very fine golf courses including Duff House Royal at Banff and Royal Tarlair at Macduff. Others, almost equally prestigious, are Buckpool, Strathlene, Cullen, Keith, Dufftown and Ballindalloch. Needless to say, the rivers Spey, Deveron, Isla, Avon, and Fiddich all offer game fishing throughout the county. There is a coastal walk all along the 30 mile length of the shore, many shorter ones often associated with interesting estates or buildings such as Duff House in Banff, and everything from a stroll around Loch Avon in the deepest Cairngorms to severely graded rock climbs on the higher peaks.

Aberdeen Angus

Straw bales

Cullen Golf Course

My and my family's love of Banffshire has spanned over five centuries and my ambition has always been to convey my love of this beautiful county to a wider audience, and to highlight all that is unique about the region.

'I Love Banffshire' shows not only the spectacular beauty of the county but also its diverse, ever-changing scenery – from the stunning coastline with its amazing Gulf Stream micro-climate to the high Cairngorms where Ben Macdhui rises to over 4,000ft. It is a treasure trove of history, from its rich maritime heritage to the magnificent architecture of its historic buildings, and the natural habitat of a wonderful variety of flora and fauna.

This book is totally unique as it is almost entirely the work of the people of Banffshire who have donated over 4,000 photographs to this project. The variety and the quality of the pictures bear testament to their deep love of their native land. Happily, I know Banffshire is secure in their lives and in their hearts, as it is in mine.

I am so grateful to you all for your kindness, interest and support. I hope very much you will enjoy this lovely photographic journey through our beloved county as much as I have.

Clare Russell. *Lord Lieutenant of Banffshire*

In awe of the majestic –
Loch Avon from the summit
of Carn Etchachan

In heaven itself, I'll ask no more than
just a Highland welcome.

Robert Burns

Any profits realised from the sale of this book
will go to Banffshire charities.

Welcome to
The Royal Burgh
of
BANFF

Banff's Arms were registered in 1672

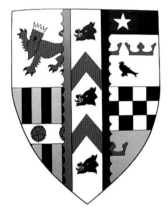

Former County Council of Banff

The Visual Identity of the County

Charles J Burnett Esq., Ross Herald of Arms

The science of heraldry is the art of visual communication. This art allows us to identify individuals, and corporate bodies such as burgh and community councils.

The former Town Council of the Royal Burgh of Banff had a registered coat of arms from 1672, and with changing forms of local government, each administration, be it County Council, District Council or Community Council, has used heraldry granted by the Lord Lyon King of Arms.

In a similar fashion individuals who lived in, or owned, parts of Banffshire can be identified through heraldry. Abercromby, Baird, Duff, Garden, Gordon, Grant, Innes, Macpherson, Ogilvy, and Sinclair, all had their unique symbols which can be found on buildings, tombs, and other items to demonstrate ownership.

In whatever form, the coats of arms of Banffshire are part of the county heritage which give identity to our particular part of the ancient realm of Scotland.

Welcome to
ABERCHIRDER

Foggieloan

Cullen Town Council

Buckie Burgh Council

Portsoy Community Council

Keith Community Council

Macduff Burgh Council

Whitehills Community Council

Portknockie Community Council

Fordyce Community Association

Dufftown Burgh Council

17

The BANFFSHIRE Coast

There are 12 charming towns and villages and 11 harbours on the 26 miles from the village of Crovie in the east to Portgordon in the west. The harvest of the sea drew people to this area, and rewards from the herring fishing of the 19th and first part of the 20th centuries provided most of the fine sandstone houses which give the towns and villages their character. Fisher seatowns like those at Findochty and the Royal Burgh of Cullen provide quaint and delightful places to explore, although the random house numbers must be a postman's nightmare.

The area has produced many sea captains, Portgordon in 1870 having 26 in a population of around 800. It is said that in the course of a year, in the 18th and 19th centuries, a passage could be taken from Portsoy to any part of the New World. The Royal Navy has been well served, and Captain Duff, from Banff, one of Nelson's top captains, killed at Trafalgar, is remembered on a memorial at Banff Castle and in Westminster Abbey.

Boat building has been part of the way of life over the past 200 years, with thousands of fishing craft being built by expert hands all along the coast. Watt of Macduff continues to build the finest craft for the fishing fleet, whilst Buckie Shipyard specialises in repairing and refitting vessels, including the RNLI's most modern lifeboats: up to five Severns may be seen there at one time.

The glory days of fishing belong to the herring fishers, every harbour having had its fleet of drifters, first under sail, then steam, and latterly diesel driven. Skippers and crews hunted the herring using a succession of ports, as the fish in the course of the year followed the drift of plankton round the coast of Britain; all the way from the southwest, north to Shetland, and ending the year off Yarmouth. Large supporting teams of women gutters, fish curers, salesmen, and tradesmen of all kinds followed the fleet; their stories are recorded at Buckie Fishing Heritage Cottage.

More efficient fishing methods have replaced the drift net; seine netting now overtaken by trawling, while purse netting has been used by men from Macduff and Gardenstown. The result is more efficiency, fewer boats and fewer men in the industry, with the extra space in many harbours giving a boost to recreational sailing. Despite modern developments, a fisherman's life remains one of extremes of danger, hardship, fortune, joy and sorrow, the measure of his success decided at the last minute by prices at the market. There is a constant cull on the lives of fishing crews, almost 200 men having been lost at sea from this area alone since the Second World War. Despite changes, fishing remains part of Banffshire, and the best of fish is processed and available to buy along the coast, not only in the towns, but also in villages like Sandend and Whitehills.

Fishermen have been called the 'last of the hunters', and this is embodied by Peter Smith, a successful Buckie skipper who moved into the 21st century by taking his boat, the Victory, first to Greenland to catch shrimps, then to south west Africa to hunt the fish of the southern Atlantic. Perhaps Peter's venture displays a shrewd insight into the future of the industry.

John Fowlie
Vice Lord Lieutenant of Banffshire

Gardenstown

Findochty by Bill Hunter

Hauling the herring nets
by Bill Hunter

The Pier at Crovie

Portknockie

Cullen Harbour

The Cullen Railway viaduct was created as a result of the Earl of Seafield's objection to the new Great North of Scotland's Railway line passing too close to Cullen House. The present town of Cullen, rebuilt around 1820, was moved from its former site by the 'Big House' at Old Cullen for similar reasons. 1886 saw the opening of the railway which linked the coastal communities of Banffshire. The arches in the picture, which are at the viaduct's western end, were built in the 1880s using steam tractors, horses, and the sweat of Irish 'navvies'. The most westerly arch gives access to Cullen Golf Course and the splendid sands of Cullen Bay.

Storm at Macduff

Banff Harbour

Buckie Harbour

Cullen Harbour

25

Portsoy Boat Festival

So Ranald rubs the peat-gold lettering that reads
Scottish Maid 1864 Port Soy
as if it were a genie's bottle
that will release his seafaring ancestors
who left him this relic of the herring heydays.
But that will not happen:
for this bell's chimes will never again
sound to mark the end of a watch,
or be furiously rung to raise an alarm;
nor will its clangs rejoice wildly
at a plentiful haul of the silver darlings.

*The Portsoy Boat Festival is a hugely popular
annual event held in this picturesque Banffshire
port, with various events and local attractions
including curing Arbroath Smokies*

The Salmon Bothy

Evening ebb-tide at Banff Links

Findochty Harbour

31

Left: Johnnie Mackenzie, Chairman of Herd and Mackenzie's shipyard, welcomes Sir Peter Scott, son of legendary polar explorer, Scott of the Antarctic, depicted as the figurehead of the vessel, being restored (right)

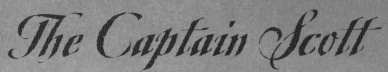

The Captain Scott

The *Captain Scott* was built by Herd & Mackenzie at Buckie in 1972. She is a topsail schooner of 150 feet, built for the Outward Bound Trust and later sold to the Sultan of Oman to be used as a sail training ship. She is still in the Gulf, painted white and renamed the *Youth of Oman.*

Clockwise from top left: rigging the vessel; in full sail; the wooden hull in construction; the proud staff of Herd & Mackenzie in 1972

Sea-Fever

I must down to the seas again, to the lonely sea and the sky,
And all I ask is a tall ship and a star to steer her by,
And the wheel's kick and the wind's song and the white sail's shaking,
And a grey mist on the sea's face, and a grey dawn breaking.

I must down to the seas again, for the call of the running tide
Is a wild call and a clear call that may not be denied;
And all I ask is a windy day with the white clouds flying,
And the flung spray and the blown spume, and the sea-gulls crying.

I must down to the seas again, to the vagrant gypsy life,
To the gull's way and the whale's way where the wind's like a whetted knife;
And all I ask is a merry yarn from a laughing fellow-rover
And quiet sleep and a sweet dream when the long trick's over.

By John Masefield (1878-1967)
(English Poet Laureate, 1930-1967)

A particularly bleak and windswept
winter view of Banff

Findochty

Portknockie

Forsyths reels for oil industry

Built by Thompson's, Buckie

36

The Villages and their Small Harbours

In earlier days, the villages with harbours shared the success of the herring fishing, and between fishings, the latter would have been packed from wall to wall with sailing boats and steam drifters.

Lobster and crab, with mackerel in summer and some cod and haddock fishing in winter, give work to a few small boats; but their numbers have dwindled to a handful, and in many small harbours fishing vessels are greatly outnumbered by leisure craft.

Despite these changes, a feeling of past history remains, like a distant echo.

Netmender

Whitehills

Sandend

Sandend

Creel Boats

37

Gamrie Parish, containing Gardenstown village, was the scene of 10th-century battles
with invading Norsemen, the skulls of some of whom were for many years built
into the walls of St John's church on the cliff overlooking the village. Gardenstown
may still be influenced by some Norse genes. In the early 20th century it was noted
for its high proportion of left-handers and children with red or ginger hair. More
recently it was considered to be a village with the highest per capita income in the UK
(proportionate to the size of the population). This was probably due to the fact that a
number of very successful fishing skippers lived there.

The once thriving fishing port of Crovie is unique in many ways, due to its inaccessibility from the land. It has no cars, but every house has its own wheelbarrow.

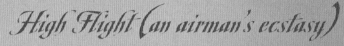

High Flight (an airman's ecstasy)

Oh, I have slipped the surly bonds of earth
And danced the skies on laughter-silvered wings;
Sunward I have climbed and joined the tumbling mirth
Of sun-split clouds – and done a hundred things
You have not dreamed of; wheeled and soared and swung
High in the sun-lit silence. Hovering there
I've chased the shouting wind along, and flung
My eager craft through footless halls of air;
Up, up the long, delirious, burning blue
I've topped the wind-swept heights with easy grace,
Where never lark nor even eagle flew;
And while, with silent lifting mind I've trod
The high untrespassed sanctity of space,
Put out my hand, and touched the face of God.

John Gillespie Magee (1922-41)

42

Sealife

The seas around Banffshire benefit from the warming influence of the Gulf Stream and the rich nutrients flowing from the Moray Firth. Combined, these factors produce a fertile environment for plankton and food for many species of cetaceans, seals and seabirds.

Below: Oystercatchers
Bottom: A feeding Minke whale is joined by gulls, guillemots and razorbills

The bottle-nosed dolphins here are part of the most northerly population in the world, and are also the largest of their species

Common seals basking

Sea anemones

43

Baiting the lines at Portknockie – late 19th century

The Fishing Industry

The former local fleet of perhaps 800 herring drifters has been replaced by a greatly diminished number of Buckie and Macduff trawlers, at the present time working mainly from the harbours at Fraserburgh and Peterhead, catching both demersal and pelagic fish.

Buckie and Macduff now host smaller landings of prawns, scallops, lobster and crab, with squid providing a summer season in recent years.

Drying the haddock

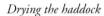

North-Easterly

I stand between the land and sea…

Mustard-bright, lichen overcoats the smudgy grey
hunch-shouldered rocks. Rock-faces endure

the rough lick of the sea,
waves rise, white-tongued,
in energetic echoes of the blue spasmodic Firth.

Look up – over this world's floodtides,

arches the wide embrace
of the clearly blue, unmoving sky.

Hilda Meers
Award-winning Whitehills poet and author

Buckie in the 1950s by Bill Hunter

Macduff Harbour

Sandend

Will there be a lobster in the creel?

Portsoy Harbour

Macduff shipyard

Gutting fish at Macduff

Macduff shipyard

45

Evocations of a wild coast

46

Macduff lifeboat

Eternal Father, strong to save
Whose arm hath bound the restless wave.
Who bidd'st the mighty ocean deep
Its own appointed limits keep
  Oh hear us when we cry to thee
  For those in peril on the sea.

From *For Those in Peril on the Sea*
(William Whiting)

The William Blannin *in fine weather…*

… and foul!

Left: RNLB Charles Brown *with its replacement The* William Blannin *(above)*

48

Buckie Shipyard

Lifeboat coming ashore on boat hoist

Macduff seawall awash during a storm

Our Heroes of the Sea

Lifeboats have put to sea from Buckie, Macduff and Whitehills for almost 150 years. The present-day commitment of the RNLI to provide help within 2 hours for vessels up to 50 miles offshore is satisfied by the presence of a 17 metre Severn all-weather lifeboat at Buckie, and Macduff's Atlantic 75. Speed of vessels and speed of communications have transformed the service, and boats are under way in from six to ten minutes of a request for launch. Although enormous technological change has taken place, one thing remains constant, and that is the willingness of the part-time voluntary crews to go to sea 24/7 in all weathers. Ordinary men and women, well trained, doing extraordinary things.

Remuneration for the crews is minimal, the customer is never charged for the service, and the RNLI is totally funded by voluntary donations from the general public. Where else in the world can you match that?

Illustration by Bill Hunter

Buckie and District Seamen's Memorial Chapel

The memorial commemorates the loss of life at sea since the Second World War, of men from the immediate coastal communities. Over 170 names are recorded on the Roll of Honour. Almost all were fishermen.

The Chapel was built in the late 19th century as a meeting place and Sunday school for the Free Church, on a site which would have been centrally placed for most of the population of the town. It later saw service as the practice venue for the famous Buckie Fishermen's Choir, then as a meeting place for the Salvation Army.

Lord, your sea is so great and my boat is so small

Portuguese fisherman's prayer

Around 1980, a group of people, some having suffered personal loss through tragedy at sea, led by Mrs Jean Hillier, convened in order to develop the Memorial. The late Alexander Wilson, architect, designed the attractive interior, and the late Charles Florence created the modern stained glass windows, depicting the way of life and reflecting the spirit of the fishing community, which today sparkle in the sunlight and fill the tiny chapel with a spectrum of colour.

The Memorial Chapel opened on 4th July 1982. The following day the Queen and Prince Phillip visited, met the organising committee and spoke to a number of bereaved families.

When those you love
become a memory,
the memory becomes
a treasure

Anon

51

RECIPES *from the* SEA

Avocados & scallops

Melts in the mouth

INGREDIENTS

2 tablespoons oil
8oz/225g queen scallops, trimmed
Garlic (optional)
2 ripe avocados, halved, stoned and
 sliced
Lettuce
1 tbsp mayonnaise (home-made if
 possible)
1 tbsp crème fraîche
Juice and zest of 1 lime/lemon
2 rashers bacon, fried and diced
Bag of herb leaves for decoration

METHOD

Heat oil in pan and toss trimmed
scallops and garlic in it for about 2
minutes till opaque. Remove and keep
warm. Halve, peel and stone avocados.
Slice lengthways and place in ear-
dishes. Shred a little lettuce and make
nest for scallops. Mix 1 tablespoon of
mayonnaise and 1 tablespoon of crème
fraîche in bowl with juice and zest of
the lime. Season. Add scallops and mix
well. Place scallops on bed of lettuce
and sprinkle with warm bacon.

Recipe for Cullen Skink

A very regional recipe

INGREDIENTS

25g/1oz margarine
4 undyed smoked haddock fillets,
 about 225g/8oz each
½ onion, chopped
4 potatoes (preferably Kerr's Pink
 or other floury variety), peeled and diced
2 tsp cornflour
1.75l/ 3 pt milk
4 tbsp single cream
salt and freshly ground black pepper

Bay of Cullen

METHOD

Melt the margarine in a large saucepan. Skin and
break haddock in large pieces. Add haddock and
onion to pan and cook gently for 2 minutes.
Par-boil potatoes until almost tender, then drain.
Mix cornflour with 1 tablespoon cold milk. Add
remaining milk and potatoes to saucepan and
bring to the boil. Stir in the cornflour and simmer
for 2 minutes.
Just before serving, stir in cream and season.

Hot avocados with prawns & bacon

An intriguing and unusual mixture

INGREDIENTS

8 slices bacon
2 avocados, halved and stoned
4 tbsp mayonnaise
1 small pkt 4oz/100g prawns
4 tbsp grated Cheddar cheese

METHOD

Fry bacon and chop. Scoop out avocados,
dice and mix with mayonnaise, bacon and
prawns. Place back in avocados, sprinkle with
cheese and bake at 400°F/200°C/Gas 6 for 10
minutes.

P.S. If you serve fish as the main course you
can swap prawns for gently fried mushrooms.

Smoked haddock mousselines with a prawn & hollandaise sauce

My favourite starter – you must try it!

INGREDIENTS

10oz/250g smoked haddock
2 eggs, lightly beaten
Salt and pepper
Nutmeg
½ pt/300ml double cream

METHOD

Skin and chop fish. Liquidise with salt, pepper and nutmeg. Blend in beaten eggs and put in fridge for a few hours. Place in liquidiser with cream and process. Butter cocotte dishes well and pour mixture into them. Stand in bain-marie (a baking tin half-filled with hot water) and bake at 375°F/190°C/Gas 5 for 30 minutes. Leave to stand for 2-3 minutes. Turn out and serve with prawn hollandaise.

Hollandaise with Prawns:
4 egg yolks
1 tbsp water
2 tbsp lemon juice
6oz/150g melted butter
4oz/100g large prawns
Salt and pepper

METHOD

Whisk egg yolks, water and lemon juice in a bowl over hot water. Pour in melted butter and whisk until thick. Add prawns and seasoning to taste.

FARMING *and* FOOD

Banffshire has an amazing diversity of farming: from the wonderful fertile land of the coast with its amazing micro-climate, to the cattle and sheep lands of the mountainous Cairngorms.

Most of the arable goes to the food chain and to bio-diesel, but the best goes to malting barley which is sold to the whisky distilleries. The Scots firmly believe we have the best lamb and beef in the world, and in Banffshire my family started, in 1860, one of the first pedigree herds of Aberdeen Angus. We are now the oldest herd in continued existence and every Aberdeen Angus steak you eat can be traced back to the Ballindalloch bloodlines.

Banffshire is also lucky enough to have the world-famous Walkers Shortbread at Aberlour, a wonderful business, still run by members of the family.

End of harvest

Ploughing match

Aberdeen Angus

Highland cow

The day has gone. And the sun has dropped, like a penny, into the pocket of the night. The noise of day is no more. And in the field there is only solitude and quiet, the cool sweet solace of evening. There is stubble on the field and it sleeps golden at the dropping of the sun. Where are you? Look, there is a pigeon in its own basketful of sky, calling and searching, as I search and call. Where are you?

Look, here is my hand held out for you. Take it. For we have a long, long way to go together. And one hand always needs another. Look how the moon has climbed above the wood, above the field, a bright new penny waiting to be found. Come then, take my hand and we will go find the moon, hand with hand together.

W. Ferrier Mavor (1913–1997)

Oats

Many generations of Banffshire 'loons and quines' were raised on this staple food which Samuel Johnson said was "a grain which in England is generally given to horses, but which in Scotland supports the people." And how right we Scots were to eat our oats, although not many of us would want to return to the days when porridge was poured into a drawer to cool at the beginning of the week and cut out in slices as the week went on!

As we know today, the humble oat, once grown on every Banffshire farm, not only provides food and bedding for animals but is also now recognised as one of the 'superfoods', full of vitamins and minerals, and with a valuable role to play in keeping the circulatory system healthy, lowering 'bad' cholesterol levels and preventing heart disease.

Porridge and oatcakes are two of the best-known oatmeal dishes, but this versatile grain has many applications and can be used as a coating for food (eg herrings rolled in oatmeal), an addition to hearty soups and stews, in bread, cakes and biscuits, or as a constituent of haggis or stuffing. Hamlyns of Boyndie are renowned for their porridge oats and are still part of a family food business spanning 14 generations of history in oat milling

Other than for culinary use, oats were at one time used as a form of currency, and had medicinal applications as well, notably in the form of poultices. Many modern beauty and skincare products include oats.

Why is there no monument to porridge in our land?

If it's good enough to eat, it's good enough to stand!

On a plinth in London, a statue we should see

Of porridge made in Scotland, signed 'Oatmeal, O.B.E'

Quote by Spike Milligan

There's always one!

Loin of lamb with an onion & fennel marmalade surrounded by whisky sauce

INGREDIENTS

2 red onions, finely sliced
1 head of fennel, finely sliced
2oz/50g butter and
    another 1oz /25g diced
1 tbsp sugar
1 loin of lamb
Rosemary
2 courgettes
Seasoning

METHOD

Sauté red onion and fennel in 1oz/25g of butter, over a
low heat until soft. Add sugar and cook for one minute.
Remove and keep warm. Slice loin diagonally. Flatten
slightly and sprinkle with rosemary. Season. Melt rest of
butter in pan and fry the slices of lamb for one minute
on each side. Remove and keep warm. Quick fry the
courgettes until hot and then slice into thin strips. Place
slices of lamb on plate and accompany with courgettes
and the onion and fennel marmalade, surrounded with a
whisky sauce.

FOR WHISKY SAUCE:
½pt/300ml double cream
1 tbsp Ballindalloch Castle malt whisky
Seasoning
Chopped parsley

METHOD
Heat cream until boiling, add whisky and season.
Sprinkle in parsley.

RECIPES *from the* FARM

Nosey Porkers

Fillet of pork with a black grape & crème fraîche sauce

These ingredients go so well together

INGREDIENTS

1lb/450g fillet of pork
2 tbsp olive oil
2 tbsp flour
Seasoning
3-4 tbsp red wine vinegar
Bunch of black grapes
2 tsp peppercorns, lightly crushed
1 x 8oz/200g pot crème fraîche
Chopped parsley for decoration

METHOD

Slice pork into about 8 pieces about 1in/2.5cm thick. Heat oil in a frying pan. Place flour in bowl and season. Add pork pieces and dust off excess. Place in frying pan and cook for about 3-4 minutes on each side. Remove from pan using a slotted spoon and keep warm. Add red wine vinegar, grapes and crushed peppercorns to pan and swirl about. Take off heat and stir in crème fraîche and chopped parsley. Return pork to pan and spoon over the sauce.

Re-heat for a few minutes. (DO NOT BOIL).
Season. Serve with ribbons of pasta and asparagus.

Crusty lamb with mangoes & walnuts

Unusual and mouthwatering

INGREDIENTS

2–3 tbsp olive oil

2 fillets of Scottish lamb – about 7oz/175g each

6oz/150g finely chopped mushrooms

1 garlic clove, finely chopped

8oz/225g coarse country pâté

1 tin mangoes (strained and chopped) plus extra for decoration

1 small pkt chopped walnuts/pecans

8oz/225g large spinach leaves

2 x 13oz/375g pkts of ready-rolled puff pastry

1 large egg, beaten

Seasoning

METHOD

Heat 2 tablespoons olive oil in frying pan. Sear lamb fillets all over till browned. Remove from pan and set aside. Fry mushrooms and garlic lightly. Remove from pan with slotted spoon and set aside. Mix together pâté, mushrooms, garlic, chopped mangoes and walnuts. Season. Wash spinach leaves and place in saucepan. Cook gently till wilted. Squeeze water out well. Cool.

Place ready-rolled pieces of puff pastry on board. Lay spinach leaves on top. Spread pâté mixture over spinach, then place fillets of lamb on each and fold into two neat parcels. Brush with beaten egg and place on baking tray. Rest in fridge for 10 minutes, then bake at 400°F/200°C/Gas 6 for 20–25 minutes till pastry is crusty and golden. Serve sliced thickly with some warmed slices of mango on the side.

Hairy tatties

Try it if you dare!

Filleted fish (both haddock and cod) used to be preserved in the coastal villages by heavily salting and drying outside in the wind – usually on the washing line. The result is similar to the bacalao as found in Portugal and other European countries, and was kept indoors in a dry cupboard or, exceptionally, under the bed!

Hairy tatties as a delicacy is something of an acquired taste. First you must soak the fish overnight and bring them to the boil, throwing away the 'bree' (some say three times). Then they are shredded into a fibrous mess. This is eaten separately with mashed potatoes, or combined with them along with milk, cream, butter, parsley and 'spice' (pepper) as available, but positively without added salt. One can still buy the dried salt fish without having to go to Portugal.

King Edward potato

Another one of Banffshire's exports are King Edwards. These are a high quality potato and are renowned for their creamy white flesh and floury texture. They very rarely discolour on cooking… Majestic!

Walkers Shortbread

The Walkers story began over a hundred years ago in 1898, when the 21-year-old Joseph Walker opened the doors of his own bakery in Torphins with a loan of £50 and the dream of making the finest shortbread in the world.

In the first year of business, Joseph used every spare moment to perfect his shortbread recipe, and it was time well spent. Soon shooting parties from the local estates were making detours to Joseph's bakery.

As his fame spread and demand increased for his quality shortbread, Joseph took the first steps to expanding the business by moving to a larger shop in the Speyside village of Aberlour and investing in a horse and cart to deliver his baking further afield.

By the 1970s, Joseph's grandchildren had begun exporting Walkers shortbread to over 60 countries around the world – still baking to his original recipe. Within a decade, they won the first of three Queen's Awards for Export Achievement – the highest accolade given to British exporters.

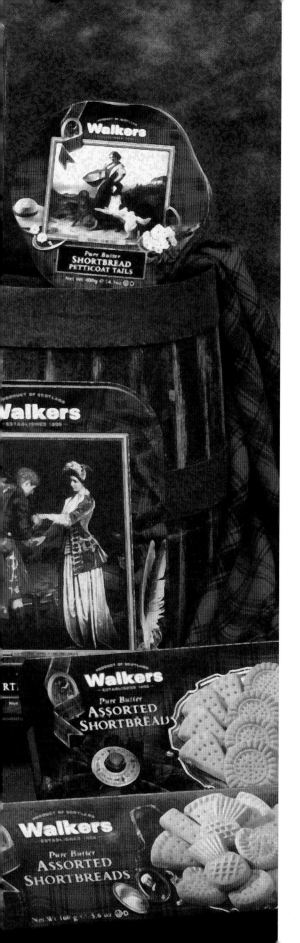

A Spey larder

WHISKY *the* WATER *of* LIFE

Traditional Oak

SHERRY WOOD

SHERRY WOOD

SHERRY WOOD

SHERRY WOOD

NEW OAK

NEW OAK

NEW OAK

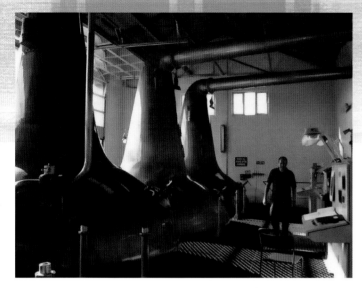

The huge copper stills are part of the whisky manufacturing process, where only the most delicate vapours rise up, condense and are drawn off. These stills at Craigellachie demonstrate just one of the many shapes and sizes they can be

The Story of Glenfiddich

A strong connection exists between the Macpherson-Grant family and the Grants of Glenfiddich. After the bloody Battle of Culloden, fought on 16th April 1746, one of the fleeing Jacobites, Alexander Grant, sought succour at his namesake's, Alexander Grant, the Laird of Ballindalloch. His appeal was granted, and the Laird found him a vacant croft called Gightcot, far up on nearby Ben Rinnes. There he could be hidden from The Duke of Cumberland's prying Dragoons scouring the area requisitioning food for the army.

William Grant, Alexander's descendant, started life as a herd-boy guarding the Duke of Fife's cattle on the hillsides in Speyside. With his wife Elizabeth by his side and his two daughters and seven sons, he rose to be the founder of what was to become William Grant & Sons, the famous Scotch whisky distillers. After 20 years of saving – the Scots are good at that! – he realised his dream of creating "the best dram in the valley". With second-hand equipment, some land acquired on Speyside, and the services of one stonemason, he and his family built the Glenfiddich Distillery with their bare hands. And on Christmas Day 1887, William Grant and Sons' Pure Malt Whisky first ran from the stills, with the entire project costing a mere £800. Encouraged by his success, several other distilleries sprang up in the area but, not to be outdone, Grant decided to expand and acquired more land and water rights. Then, like an implausible Hollywood plot line, he acquired his master's castle of Balvenie, which he converted to his second distillery!

A Scottish fairy-tale come true if ever there was one.

Give me the real Glenlivet... The human mind never tires o' Glenlivet... if a body could just find out the exac' proper proportion and quantity that ought to be drunk every day, and keep to that, I verily trow that he might leave for ever, without dying at a', and that doctors and kirkyards would go out o' fashion.

An illicit still at Glenfarclas

Scotch whisky is first recorded as far back as 1494, when it is referred to in accounts of King James IV of Scotland, but its traditions and indeed its manufacture undoubtedly go much further back. To the Highlanders of old, nothing seemed more natural than to use the good clear water, surplus barley, the plentiful peat and the inherited skills of the 'cunning chemicals' to produce *Uisge beatha* the 'water of life'.

The Speyside Cooperage

*I*n the heart of Scotland's rolling hills lies Speyside Cooperage, the only working cooperage in the UK where you can experience the ancient art of coopering.

Since 1947, the family owned Speyside Cooperage has produced the finest casks from the best American Oak. Today the cooperage continues to work and produce the age-old product, still using traditional methods and tools. Although shipped across the world, many of the casks remain in Scotland, providing a vital ingredient in Scotland's whisky-making process.

At Speyside Cooperage they rely on oak as this is the only wood that can be used to produce casks for quality wines and spirits, as it prevents seepage and allows the contents to breathe without spoiling the flavour.

There are over 50 species of oak growing throughout the world but only a few are suitable for coopering. It can take 100–150 years before the oak required is ready for harvesting, at which time it is specially selected for their casks, which can last up to 50 years.

Firing the casks

71

The Malts of Banffshire

Whisky – the water of life

1 Aberlour
2 Aultmore
3 Auchroisk
4 Allt-a-Bhainne
5 Balvenie
6 Braeval
7 Benrinnes
8 Cragganmore
9 Craigellachie
10 Dailuaine
11 Dufftown
12 Glendullan
13 Glenfiddich
14 Glenallachie
15 Glentauchers
16 Glenfarclas
17 Glenlivet
18 Glen Keith
19 Glenglassaugh
20 Inchgower
21 Knockdhu (An Cnoc)
22 Macduff (Glen Deveron)
23 Mortlach
24 Pittyvaich
25 Strathisla
26 Strathmill
27 Tamnavulin
28 Tomintoul

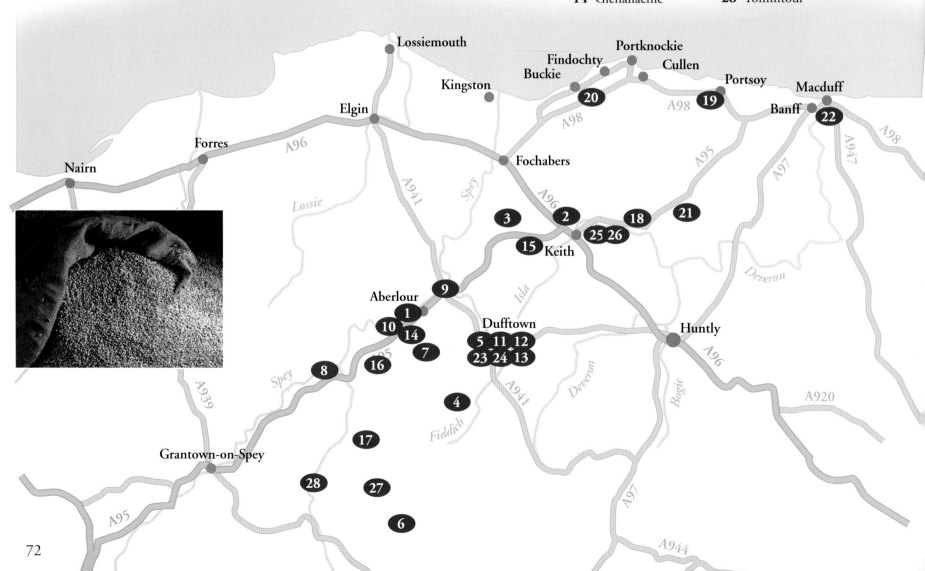

Scotch on the rocks

73

From *I Love Food*
by Clare Russell

Highland bread & butter pudding (Kenny's secret recipe)

The best bread and butter pudding

INGREDIENTS
2oz/50g softened butter
3oz/75g raisins
3oz/75g sultanas
3 tbsp whisky
12 slices brioche bread
1oz/25g heather honey
8 egg yolks
5oz/125g caster sugar
300ml milk
300ml double cream
2 tsp vanilla essence
2 tbsp demerara sugar
Icing sugar for dusting
Apricot glaze (4oz apricot jam boiled with
    2oz water to make a hot sticky glaze)

METHOD
Grease a 3 pint pudding dish with butter. Soak the raisins and sultanas in the whisky for 4 hours. Spread each slice of bread with the softened butter and a mere scraping of heather honey. Remove the crusts and cut in half diagonally twice creating 4 triangles per slice. Arrange the bread in layers in the prepared oven-proof dish scattering the raisins and sultanas between the layers.

Whisk the egg yolks and caster sugar together. Bring the milk and cream to the simmer. Pour the hot cream mixture over the egg yolks and sugar mixture. Add the vanilla essence. You now have a custard. Pour the custard over the bread and sprinkle with demerara sugar. Bake in a bain-marie (a baking tin half-filled with hot water) in a pre-heated oven at 350F/180C/Gas 4 for 20–30 minutes until the pudding begins to set. When ready remove from the water bath. Dust with some icing sugar and glaze under the grill on medium heat.

Make the apricot glaze by boiling the apricot jam and water together. Brush a thin coating of glaze over the top of the pudding. It is now ready to serve.

Ballindalloch haggis mousselines with a whisky, cream & onion sauce

A tasty Scottish dish that has to be tried

INGREDIENTS
6oz/150g turnip
6oz/150g creamed potatoes
8oz/225g haggis
Seasoning
Finely chopped parsley and chives for decoration

For sauce:
1 generous glass Glenfiddich whisky
½pt/300ml double cream
1 finely sliced onion

METHOD

Cook turnip and mash with a little butter and seasoning. Cook potatoes and mash well (no lumps) with a little butter and seasoning. Cook haggis by wrapping in foil and placing in oven 350ºF/180ºC/Gas 4 for about 45 minutes. Assemble mousselines by layering turnip, haggis and lastly creamed potato into buttered ramekins. Place ramekins in bain-marie (roasting tin half-filled with boiling water) and bake at 350ºF/180ºC/Gas 4 for about 20–25 minutes. Meanwhile, make whisky sauce. Heat whisky in pan, take off heat and ignite. Pour in double cream and finely chopped onion and heat till boiling point. Keep warm.

To serve, take mousselines out of oven, run knife round edge of them and invert onto plate. Drizzle with whisky sauce and sprinkle with finely chopped parsley and chives.

For Chef: a dram of whisky

The noble haggis

Ballindalloch 'Ericas', 1884,
by David George Steell

Aberdeen Angus is the best. The pedigree herd was started by my great-grandfather, Sir George Macpherson-Grant of Ballindalloch, in 1860. It is now the oldest herd in existence. Interestingly, Sir George, with his friend, John Smith, founded the Cragganmore Distillery.

Ballindalloch beef tournedos with a Cragganmore whisky cream sauce

INGREDIENTS

2oz/50g butter
2 Aberdeen Angus fillet steaks about
    1in/2.5cm thick
1 finely chopped onion
4oz/100g sliced mushrooms
1 tbsp Cragganmore whisky
¼ pt/150ml cream
2 tsp chopped parsley
2 rounds of fried bread
2oz/50g pâté

METHOD

Melt butter in pan and cook steaks until
done as desired. Remove from pan and
keep warm. Fry onion and mushrooms
in pan with butter. Add whisky, cream,
chopped parsley and seasoning. Simmer
for a few minutes. Spread fried bread
round with pâté.
Place beef on
round and serve
whisky sauce
separately.

Shooting AND Stalking

Banffshire is renowned for its superb variety of shooting, stalking and fishing.

Sportsmen from all over the world come to partake of its pleasures and pursuits.

Looking over to Ben Rinnes

These are my mountains

For fame and for fortune I wandered the earth
And now I've come back to the land of my birth
I've bought back my treasures but only to find
They're less than the pleasures I first left behind.

For these are my mountains and this is my glen
The braes of my childhood will know me again
No land's ever claimed me tho' far I did roam
For these are my mountains and I'm going home.

The burn by the road sings at my going by
The whaup overhead wings with welcoming cry
The loch where the scart flies at last I can see
It's here that my heart lies, it's here I'll be free.

For these are my mountains and this is my glen
The braes of my childhood will know me again
No land's ever claimed me tho' far I did roam
For these are my mountains and I'm going home.

Kind faces will meet me and welcome me in
And how they will greet me my ain kith and kin
The night round the ingle the old songs will be sung
At last I'll be hearing my ain mother tongue.

For these are my mountains and this is my glen
The braes of my childhood will know me again
No land's ever claimed me tho' far I did roam
For these are my mountains and I'm going home.

James Copeland

Ballindalloch Estate gamekeepers
and ghillies in the Estate tweed

Song of Solomon

My beloved is like a gazelle
or a young stag.
Look, there he stands behind our wall,
gazing in at the windows,
looking through the lattice.
My beloved speaks and says to me:
'Arise, my love, my fair one, and come away;
For now the winter is past,
the rain is over and gone.
The flowers appear on the earth;
The time of singing has come,
and the voice of the turtle dove
is heard in our land.
The fig tree puts forth its figs,
and the vines are in blossom;
they give forth fragrance.
Arise, my love, my fair one,
and come away.'

RECIPES *from the* MOORS

Roast Ballindalloch grouse

A real treat

INGREDIENTS

2oz/50g butter
4 grouse (plucked and drawn by the butcher
 – a nightmare doing it yourself!)
4 rashers rindless streaky bacon
Seasoning
4 pieces fried bread
Country pâté (home-made or bought)
Cranberry sauce

METHOD

Place dot of butter inside each bird. Cover with
bacon and place in roasting pan. Season and
dot with rest of butter. Roast at 375ºF/190ºC/
Gas 5 for about 35 minutes, basting once or
twice during cooking. Meanwhile, make fried
bread and spread with pâté. Place birds on top
and accompany with gravy, bread sauce, game
chips and cranberry sauce.

Mustardy pheasant breasts

An interesting and unusual pheasant recipe

INGREDIENTS

2 pheasant breasts
3oz/75g butter
4 tsp French mustard
1 tbsp white wine vinegar
1 dssp tarragon vinegar
2 tbsp double cream
Seasoning
Cayenne pepper

METHOD

Place pheasant breasts on foil and dot with
1oz/25g of butter. Season and wrap in foil. Bake
at 400ºF/200ºC/Gas 6 for about 15–20 minutes.
Meanwhile make sauce by melting remaining
butter in a bowl sitting in boiling water. Stir in
mustard, then wine vinegar and tarragon vinegar.
Cook for eight minutes, then add cream and
seasoning. Place pheasant breasts in a serving
dish and pour over the sauce. Sprinkle with
cayenne pepper and serve with couscous and
mange-touts.

Ballindalloch venison casserole with apricots & chestnuts

A very special combination

INGREDIENTS

2lbs/900g venison or roe deer cut into
    1in/2.5cm cubes
3–4 tbsp sunflower oil
2 onions, skinned and finely sliced
1½ pts/900ml game stock
1 tbsp redcurrant jelly
¼ pt/150ml port or red wine
1 x 15oz/400g tin whole chestnuts
1 pkt dried apricots (chopped)
Seasoning

METHOD

Toss cubed venison in two tablespoons
seasoned flour. Heat oil in pan and fry meat
till brown.

Take out of pan and leave. Add sliced onions
to pan and cook till soft. Replace meat into
pan with onions, stir in stock, redcurrant jelly,
wine, chestnuts and dried apricots.

Stir till boiling point, then place in covered
casserole and cook at 350ºF/180ºC/Gas 4 for
1–1½ hours. Serve with mashed potatoes and
purée of turnip.

Working Dogs
– Gun dogs

I had to add these two pages as the loves of my life are my 'pocket rockets' (cocker spaniels)! Dogs have always been part of country life, and are essential to shooting, farming and vermin control in the country.

Sportsmen come from all over the world to enjoy a day of driven grouse or high pheasants on the hills and glens of Strathspey. Without the beaters and pickers-up there would be no day. Anyway, half the enjoyment of the shooting is in seeing the gundogs working.

Terriers also have their uses for hunting foxes and vermin. The Norfolk terrier is not just a pretty face; it is an expert 'ratter'!

Man's best friend has always been a part of the way of life for the farmer, and no less so now. Although the quad bike has tried to take over, it still does not fulfil all the functions of a sheepdog; for a start, sheepdogs don't break down, and they don't need diesel! Border collies not only guard and control the flock, but they are also loyal, hard-working and loving.

Josie & Thomas's special treats – a doggy bribe!

Take a pound of liver (any kind) and an egg. Liquidise in a blender or food processor and add enough flour to make a stiff, scone-like mixture. Spread out in a Swiss roll tin and bake at 350°F/ 180°C /Gas 4 for about 20 minutes in a fan, or 30 minutes in a regular, oven. Ends up looking like rather solid chocolate cake. Cut into strips and freeze, taking out when needed.

Unfortunately, in the making of it the smell is somewhat overpowering and lingering, so we suggest you make it outside!

Working Dogs – Sheep Dogs

88

Fishing

Scottish Angler's Lament

Sometimes ower early,
Sometimes ower late,
Sometimes nae water,
Sometimes a spate,
Sometimes ower dirty,
Sometimes ower clear,
There's aye something wrang,
When I'm fishing here.

Lord give me grace
To catch a fish
So large that even I,
When talking of it
Afterwards,
May never need
To lie

*Ballindalloch Ghillie,
Steve Brand, and one of the
fishers with his catch*

Jim Walker Snr with his 28lb salmon caught at Ballindalloch

*Headstone at Lower Shaw Pool, on the Deveron, commemorating
Clementina (Tiny) Morison, 1875–1966, 'In dedication to the lady
who caught the record heaviest fresh-water salmon ever caught on a
fly in Britain October 21 1924 weight 61lb'*

91

George Michael

George Michael was Head 'Ghillie' at the Ballindalloch Estate for over 30 years. He was a hugely experienced 'Spey Caster' and greatly respected on the River Spey as a result.

He also suggested the name 'Spey' for the Rolls-Royce engines, designed over 30 years ago.

He had read in the newspapers that Rolls-Royce were asking for ideas for names for what was then the fastest engine in the world.

George suggested the name 'Spey' after the fastest flowing river in the UK.

Spey engines are still in service today, powering seven ship Classes including the Royal Navy's Type-23 Frigates.

The River Spey is the home of Spey casting and one of Scotland's big four salmon rivers. It has the third largest drainage area after the Tay and Tweed and is the second longest after the Tay. However, its major attraction is its size and the strength of its stream. In the middle and lower river it falls on average 12 feet per mile – the greatest of any British river. The river is snow fed from the Cairngorm Mountains and in a good year this can mean the river staying high until early June.

My Mistress

The River is my mistress;
I know her every mood;
She seldom smiles upon me
The sedulously wooed:
Tempestuous rage may shake her;
She may be cold and still;
Never can I forsake her
Although she use me ill.

The River is my mistress;
How ardently I strain
To win her grace and favour,
How often strive in vain
She teases me, she taunts me,
Denies my dearest wish,
And all too rarely grants me
The glory of a fish

My River is a mistress,
Not easy of access;
A thousand noes she answers
For every grudging yes.
For all that she may treat me
With scornful disregard,
Not always does she beat me.
I flog her pretty hard.

By L N Jackson

The River Spey at Craigellachie Bridge

Craigellachie Bridge

This is Scotland's oldest surviving iron bridge, built by Dumfries-born Thomas Telford and completed in 1814. It was cast in sections at an iron works in North Wales and transported by sea to the mouth of the Spey, from where it was taken by horse-drawn wagons to Craigellachie. The bridge saw many years of service, and withstood the floods of 1829 when the Spey rose 6 metres; it was renovated in 1964, and by-passed by a new bridge 8 years later, in 1972.

The commanding officers and colour parties of the Gordon Highlanders and the Queen's Own Highlanders met on Craigellachie bridge in 1994 in a show of unity before being amalgamated into the new regiment of The Highlanders. A plaque was fitted to the bridge parapet to commemorate this event.

The Deveron

RECIPES *from the* RIVER

'The Banks o' Deveron Water'

Her cheeks are like the crimson rose
Her countenance an admiration
I could not have a better choice
If I had searched o'er all the nation.

Alexander Leslie's ballad to Helen Christie (1636)

Smoked salmon & quails' egg tartlets

INGREDIENTS

4 savoury tartlet cases (make or buy)
12 quails' eggs
4oz/100g sliced smoked salmon

For hollandaise:

4 egg yolks
1 tbsp water
2 tbsp lemon juice
6oz/150g melted butter
Salt & pepper
A little dill for decoration

METHOD

Place tartlets in oven to warm. Meanwhile, make hollandaise: whisk egg yolks, water and lemon juice in a bowl over hot water. Pour in melted butter in steady stream and whisk till thick. Season. Keep warm. Poach quails' eggs in hot water with a little vinegar for about 1–1½ minutes. When cooked, but still soft, take out with slotted spoon and place on kitchen paper till dry. Place smoked salmon in tartlets, with eggs in middle and pour hollandaise over the top. Sprinkle with dill. Serve immediately

Tip: If hollandaise curdles, throw in an ice cube and beat like mad!

Egg & salmon parcels with a hollandaise & cucumber sauce

Delicious – well worth the effort

INGREDIENTS

3oz/75g long grain rice
½ pt/300ml fish stock
12oz/350g fillets of salmon
Juice of ½ lemon
2 tsp curry powder
1 tbsp fresh dill, chopped
Seasoning
15oz/425g puff pastry
6 small eggs (medium-boiled, peeled and cooled)
1 small egg, beaten

Hollandaise & cucumber sauce:

4 egg yolks
1 tbsp water
2 tbsp lemon juice
6oz/150g melted butter
½ cucumber, peeled and diced
Seasoning

METHOD

Cook rice in fish stock. Drain and cool. Place salmon in large saucepan and cover with cold water. Gently heat till simmering point and poach for 8–10 minutes till flaky. Cool. Remove bones and skin and flake fish into rice. Add lemon juice, curry powder, herbs and seasoning. Mix well. Roll out pastry into 6 x 6in (15cm) squares. Brush edges with beaten egg. Place spoonful of rice and fish mixture into middle of each square. Push eggs into centre and top with a little more of rice and fish mixture, Pull over pastry corners to middle to form square parcel, pressing joins together firmly to seal. Brush parcels with more beaten egg. Place on baking sheet and bake at 425°F/220°C/Gas 7 for about 20 minutes. Reduce oven to 375°F/190°C/Gas 5 and cook for further 10 minutes. Meanwhile, make sauce. Whisk egg yolks, water and lemon juice in bowl over hot water. Pour in melted butter and whisk till thick. Season. Fold in diced cucumber. Serve parcels accompanied with warm hollandaise and cucumber sauce.

Our FAUNA and FLORA

The heath spotted-orchid is one of the botanical stars of our local flora; the osprey holds that status amongst our fauna.

The Wild Wonders of Banffshire by Mark Hamblin, wildlife photographer extraordinaire

Stretching from sea to summit, the elongated county of Banffshire holds a multitude of habitats rich in wildlife and botanical interest. To the south-west, Banffshire dips its toes into the mighty summits of the Cairngorms where golden eagles hunt for mountain hare and ptarmigan, a member of the grouse family. Snow buntings breed in small numbers amongst the boulder fields of remote corries whilst the flatter tops hold breeding dotterel in spring.

The magnificent Glen Avon carved out by glacial activity leads down from the high tops onto a vast expanse of rolling moorland that comes alive each August as the heather blooms, attracting bees and other insects. Home to the highly-prized red grouse, the moors also provide ideal habitat for a host of upland species that include golden plover, curlew, ring ouzel, whinchat and the diminutive merlin, a dashing falcon that preys on meadow pipits.

Moorland gives way to a pastoral landscape through the county's interior, a mosaic of open fields, dry stone walls, hedgerows and woodland that supports a diversity of lowland species. Brown hares make use of the open habitat, whilst badgers, foxes and roe deer patrol the woodland edges. Yellowhammer, twite and other finches feed on spilt seed crops during the winter months alongside flocks of geese.

As the birchwoods burst into life in May they resonate to the songs of willow warblers, tree pipits, redstarts and spotted flycatchers, and host breeding tawny owls, buzzards and sparrowhawks. The region's pinewoods comprise of stands of old Caledonian forest and maturing plantations where you'll find red squirrels, crested tit and Scottish crossbill amongst its residents.

Left, from top to bottom: one oyster catcher and three grouse; the red, the capercaillie and the blackcock

99

Clockwise from top left: a puffin (sometimes called the sea parrot for obvious reasons) with its customary food of sand eels; a grey seal with its pup; the elusive otter; one of the most difficult mammals to see, the retiring pine marten

Flowing through this varied landscape, the region's many rivers and streams hold good stocks of fish including the king of fish, the Atlantic salmon, as well as freshwater crayfish and waterside birds – dipper, grey wagtail, common sandpiper, goosander and the occasional kingfisher.

Red squirrel

The Banffshire coast with its expansive views over the Moray Firth begins in the west at Spey Bay, a great place to watch ospreys hunting for fish and bottle-nosed dolphins breaching. Troup Head forms the eastern boundary of this important coastline and is one of only two mainland gannet colonies in Britain. This RSPB reserve also contains significant populations of fulmars, shags, kittiwakes, guillemots, razorbills and even a handful of comical puffins. In total over 150,000 seabirds are present here in summer.

From late summer through to early spring Banffshire's coast boasts an impressive array of wading birds that includes turnstone, redshank, oystercatcher, dunlin, curlew, knot, bar-tailed godwit and purple sandpiper. Offshore, large flocks of red-throated divers gather in autumn and great northern divers are regular in spring. Sea ducks include scoters, long-tailed ducks and eider and there is always a chance of unusual migrants to spot at almost any time of year.

Two predators ready for action: the endangered wild cat – one of the most secretive and localised of our wild creatures – and the increasingly successful peregrine falcon, one of the world's fastest flying birds

Local Rarities

On the high moors the hen harrier can be seen hunting, using the newer conifer plantations lower down as nesting sites. The female (left), is essentially brown, while the male is silver grey and white.

The stunning crested tit (right) has its UK stronghold in the remaining areas of Banffshire's ancient Caledonian forest. They can also be found in localised areas of Speyside and Deeside.

You have to be bats to live here!

In an effort to preserve an indigenous population of pipistrelle bats, this Superior Detached Residence has recently been erected for their comfort and convenience!

So, if the flight of a bird is so beautiful,

So strange and so sweet,

How more beautiful yet must be the flight
of the soul toward God,

What a glory and a sweeping on the wind

Of the wings of the spirit toward light.

Dorothea Eastwood

103

Wildfowl

Banffshire has a wide variety of habitats which support large numbers of wildfowl, both in the winter and summer. In winter the coast attracts sea duck such as long-tailed duck, scoters and mergansers, and the stubble fields hold large numbers of geese. Several species breed in the area such as the teal and birds such as the eider can be seen in harbours all year-round. The eider is interesting in that it loses its power of flight during the breeding season.

Pink-footed geese in flight

Male eider duck

Cock teal

The Swan

Mary Oliver

Did you too see it, drifting, all night, on the black river?
Did you see it in the morning, rising into the silvery air -
An armful of white blossoms,
A perfect commotion of silk and linen as it leaned
into the bondage of its wings; a snowbank, a bank of lilies,
Biting the air with its black beak?
Did you hear it, fluting and whistling
A shrill dark music – like the rain pelting the trees – like a waterfall
Knifing down the black ledges?
And did you see it, finally, just under the clouds -
A white cross streaming across the sky, its feet
Like black leaves, its wings like the stretching light of the river?
And did you feel it, in your heart, how it pertained to everything?
And have you too finally figured out what beauty is for?
And have you changed your life?

Flora

Merrily, merrily shall
I live now,
under the blossom that
hangs on the bough

William Shakespeare, *The Tempest*

The rare twinflower

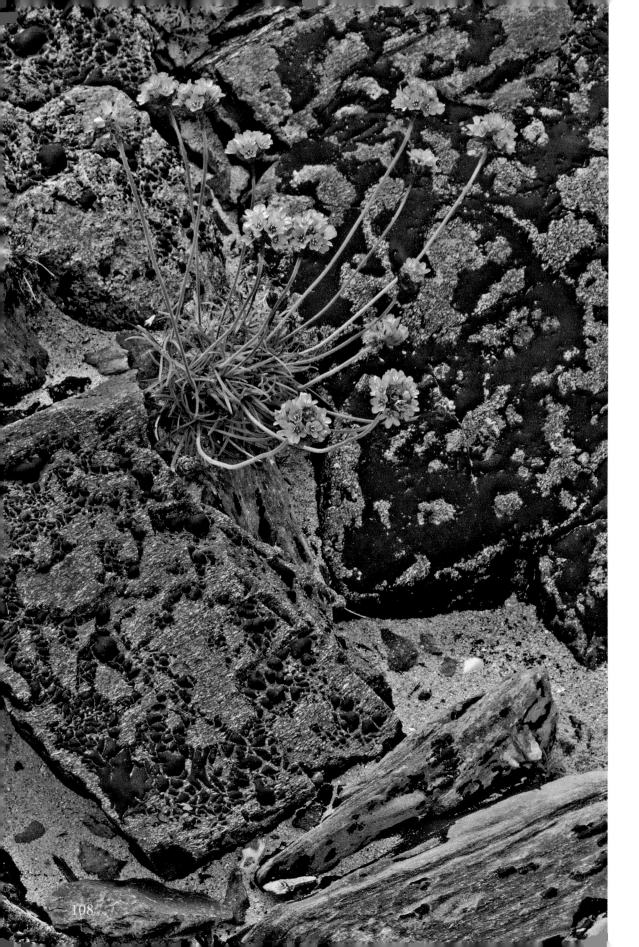

Primroses known as 'spinkies' in Banffshire

The 'Banffshire' daffodil

*'The Banffshire flower' —
dark red helleborine.*

Moorland heather not only provides an annual spectacle in August, it also supports a complex eco-system of other plants, animals and birds.

Many estates benefit economically from their grouse shooting, attracting visitors from around the world.

Further down the valleys, broom is a common, but an equally spectacular, sight with its bright yellow flowers.

HIGHLAND
Berries

Nectarines with raspberry sauce

Wonderfully easy

INGREDIENTS

8 good nectarines

Raspberry sauce

2lb/1kg raspberries/strawberries

4oz/100g caster sugar

METHOD

Halve, stone and slice nectarines. Place in a circle on a pretty glass plate.

Liquidise raspberries/strawberries and sugar, sieve and pour over nectarines before serving. Serve with whipped cream or Greek yogurt.

Scottish berry brûlée

Irresistible

INGREDIENTS

1lb/450g strawberries

8oz/225g raspberries

4oz/100g blueberries

2 tbsp caster sugar

Grated zest and juice of 1 orange

7oz/175g Greek yogurt

7floz/180ml tub of crème fraîche

3 tbsp soft brown sugar

Few pinches ground cinnamon

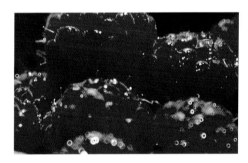

METHOD

Place strawberries, raspberries and blueberries in oven-proof dish. Sprinkle over 1 tbsp of caster sugar and grated zest and juice of 1 orange. Mix together yogurt, crème fraîche and remaining caster sugar. Spread over fruit and leave in fridge for 2 hours. Sprinkle demerara sugar and cinnamon over top and place under grill till sugar melts. Serve immediately.

The Rose Garden at Ballindalloch

O, my Luve's like a red, red rose,
That's newly sprung in June.
O, my Luve's like a melodie
That's sweetly play'd in tune.

Robert Burns

Rose bavarois with fresh raspberries

INGREDIENTS

6 egg yolks
4oz/100g caster sugar
1 tbsp cornflour
1pt/600ml milk
¾pt/450ml single cream
4 tsp powdered gelatine
   (dissolved in 3 tbsp hot water)
10 red rose petals and extra for decoration
1–2 tbsp rose water
½pt/300ml double cream
8oz/225g fresh raspberries

METHOD

Beat egg yolks with sugar, cornflour and
a little milk. Place rest of milk and single
cream in pan and bring to the boil. Pour
over egg yolk mixture, whisking constantly,
then return to pan. Cook gently till
thickened – do not boil. Strain custard
into large bowl and stir in gelatine. Set
bowl over iced water to cool mixture. Stir
occasionally till beginning to set. Chop
the rose petals finely and stir into cooked
mixture with the rose water. Lightly whip
double cream and fold into rose bavarois.
Turn into shallow soufflé dish and chill for
several hours. Unmould, decorate around
the edge with fresh
raspberries and
sprinkle with extra
red rose petals.

Let's have FUN!

Street party at Crovie

Young cellists

In this chapter we show you some of the diverse and fun activities we have in Banffshire, from our Highland Games to canoeing, surfing, skipping, dancing and skiing.

In the old days each town and village held their own Games each year, mainly so that all the communities could get together and compete against each other. The locals would walk miles to take part in their Games, and it would be the only time in the year that they would meet up with their friends and have a dram. They would toss the caber, join in a friendly tug-of-war, pipe in the massed bands and enjoy many athletic competitions. Even today Highland Games are a great attraction, not only to the locals but to the tourists also.

Canoeing and white-water rafting are very popular sports on the rivers, and of course skiing is one of the major winter sports of the county.

Mud, glorious mud!

Wet and wild!

SKIP *to* *the* BEAT *!*

Skip2TheBeat is Scotland's first competitive skipping club, and their fast feet and excellent rope-turning skills have seen these Portsoy youngsters win the British Rope Skipping Championships.

Rope Skipping on CD Now Available

'Flowers of Scotland!....Skip 2 the Beat from Portsoy show off their fantastic clutch of 34 medals from the British Rope Skipping Association championships. Back, from left: Robyn McKay, Shelby Fittall, Isla Matheson, Soricha Cameron, Meghan McKay and Ursula Jackson. Front: Stephanie Smith, Hannah Beattie and Anya Matheson.

Medal girls jump for joy

NINE youngsters from Portsoy won an amazing 34 medals at a UK skipping championship at the weekend.

Skip 2 The Beat virtually swept the boards at the British Rope Skipping Association speed competition in Birmingham, with all the girls winning medals.

Their dominance over teams from London, Birmingham and Hull left organisers commenting that they would have to come to Scotland with the event in the future.

The successful girls were Hannah Beattie (10), Soricha Cameron (13), Shelby Fittall (11), Ursula Jackson (12), Anya Matheson (11), Isla Matheson (13), Meghan McKay (13), Robyn McKay (12) and Stephanie Smith (9).

Robyn and Ursula won five medals, and Isla four – all at national level – but every

BY KEVIN DUGUID

girl in the team won a medal.

In total, they collected 16 golds, eight silver and 10 bronze in four events – speed, double-under, speed pairs and double under pairs.

In the double under contests, the rope has to pass twice under the skipper in each jump.

AMAZING

Seven of the girls had never competed at this level before, and they won 28 medals, including the top three places in all events in the novices section, and then competed in the nationals later in the day.

Isla Matheson and Megan McKay, who competed last year, lined up in the nationals and won six medals. Meghan's success was all

the more remarkable as she hurt her thumb when a dart board fell on it.

Club coach Silvanna Matheson said: "When they went up for their medals, I thought my heart was going to burst. I was cheering them on, and was so proud of every one of them.

"They had a great time, and were so excited. It was absolutely fantastic.

"They were just amazing, but they work hard and had practised like mad – but this was far more than we ever expected."

As Skip 2 the Beat, going less than three years, are the only club of their kind in Scotland, they were all kitted out in Scotland T-shirts and competed under the Saltire.

The girls were also among the medals in their first attempt at the BRSA speed competition last year, and struck gold again in the British Masters in the autumn.

116

Phone box cramming

Here, they turned their gymnastic skills to another use in an attempt to squash as many members as possible into the famous telephone kiosk at Pennan, which featured in the hit film *Local Hero*. Incredibly, it took just a couple of minutes for 16 girls to cram themselves in, breaking the existing record of 14. Unfortunately, the Guinness Book of World Records has refused to recognise the feat because they say there is no standard size for a telephone box.

The girls were promised an Easter egg each for their efforts, but the organisers ensured they were handed out AFTER the event!

HIGHLAND *Fun* and GAMES

Keith Show

Tossing the caber

Tug o' war

Many towns hold hugely competitive Highland Games events with traditional music, dancing and sports

The Keith Railway

The Keith and Dufftown Railway ('The Whisky Line') is an 11-mile heritage line linking the world's malt whisky capital, Dufftown, via Drummuir, to the market town of Keith.

The line, which was reopened by volunteers during 2000 and 2001, has 42 bridges including the famous 60ft-high two-span Fiddich Viaduct.

The track passes through some of Scotland's most picturesque scenery, with forest and farmland, lochs and glens, castles and distilleries; abundant wildlife can be glimpsed from the train, including deer, foxes, buzzards, heron, and much more.

Historic Scotland protects Tarlair open-air pool at Macduff

The wonderfully art deco Tarlair swimming pool, set in a rocky bay to the east of Macduff, is one of only three surviving seaside outdoor swimming pool complexes in Scotland, and is thought to be the finest example of its kind. Opened in the summer of 1931, the concrete-built complex comprised a tidal swimming pool, paddling and boating pools, along with changing rooms and kiosks, and curving walkways. At one time a major attraction in the North East, for residents and visitors alike, the pool sadly fell victim to the lure of the foreign package holiday, and since the 1990s the local model boat club has been the only regular user of the facility. To the delight of many, the complex, which was on the Buildings at Risk Register for Scotland, has now been categorised as Macduff's first Grade 1 listed building.

TARLAIR SWIMMING POOL, MACDUFF.   A. 2414.

An early version of a modern infinity pool

Lairig Ghru

Cairngorms from Braes of Abernethy

Loch-an-Eilein

Loch A'an, (Avon)

The Cairngorms National Park

The Cairngorms was made a National Park in September 2003 because it is a unique and special place that needs to be cared for – both for the wildlife and countryside it contains and for the people who live in it, manage it and visit it. It is Britain's largest National Park, and the southern-most part of Banffshire, including Loch Avon and Ben Macdhui, lies within it.

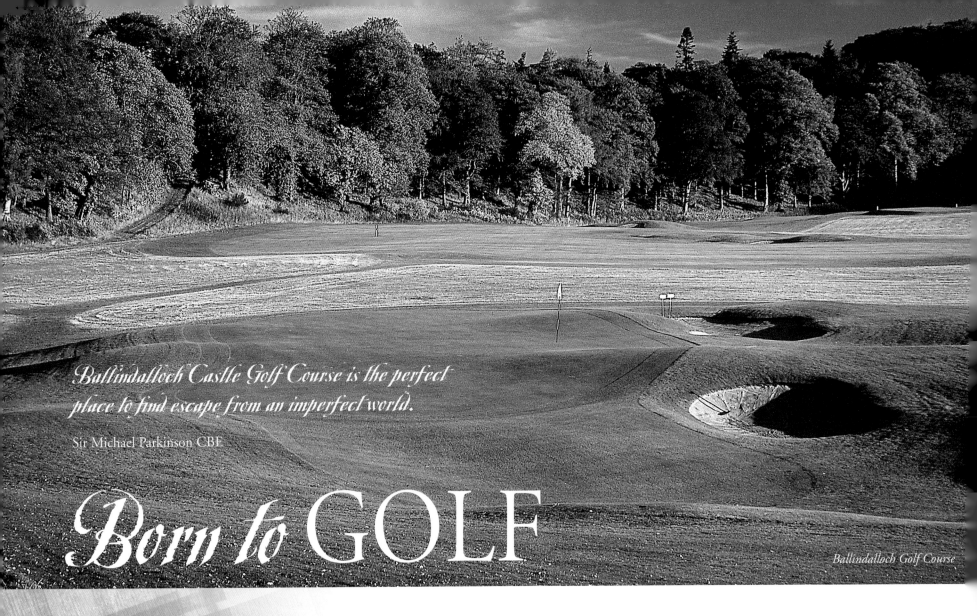

Ballindalloch Castle Golf Course is the perfect place to find escape from an imperfect world.

Sir Michael Parkinson CBE

Born to GOLF

Ballindalloch Golf Course

Scotland is the home of golf, and has some of the most beautiful and challenging courses in the world. Banffshire has great pride in its eight golf courses, which are scenic and unique.

Starting with Royal Tarlair situated in the town of Macduff, this course is renowned for its rugged beauty and panoramic views of the coastline. It is a cliff-top parkland course which presents a challenge for the more serious golfer, with the famous hole being the 13th 'Clivet' hole.

Moving on to Banff, Duff House Royal Golf Course is bounded by the River Deveron which provides a hazard for those who wander off the tee at the 7th, 9th, 16th and 17th holes. The course was re-designed in 1923 by the brilliant golf architect Dr Alister Mackenzie of 'Augusta National' fame.

Further to the west, we come to Cullen Golf Course, a traditional Scottish links course with magnificent views over the Moray Firth where dolphins are seen regularly. The club was founded in 1870 and the first nine holes close to the cliffs were laid out by Old Tom Morris. It was subsequently upgraded to 18 holes by Charlie Neaves.

Moving west again, we come to Strathlene and Buckpool golf courses, both of which are charming seaside links courses.

We now head south to Keith Golf Course, situated at the heart of the Scottish Malt Whisky Trail. The stunning Scottish scenery and the challenging parkland course provides some superb golf for experts and novices alike.

2nd Green at Dufftown

Further south we come to the Dufftown course where visitors enjoy golf in this beautiful Banffshire setting, where two of the holes feature in 'Britain's 100 Extraordinary Golf Holes'. The ninth tee is the highest golf hole in Britain, at 1,294 feet above sea level. All holes have different playing tactics due to the undulation of the course. Overall, the experience is of rolling fairways lined with heather and heath.

Finally we come to the charming new nine-hole, 18-tee golf course at Ballindalloch, nestling amidst mature trees on the banks of the River Avon. Designed by David Steel, the course has a par of 72 and gives fishermen excellent sport when river conditions on the Spey and Avon are not favourable.

Photograph by Charles Lindsay from his book 'Lost Balls'

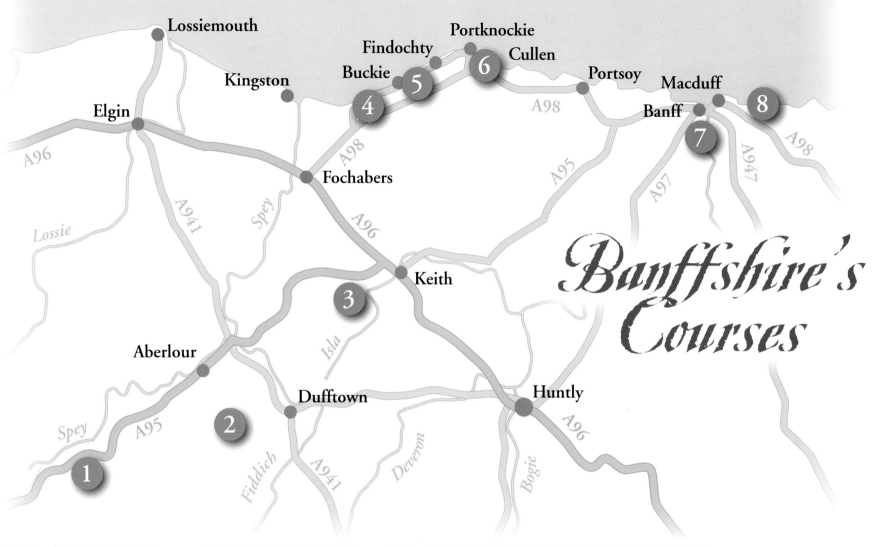

Lossiemouth

Portknockie

Findochty Cullen

Kingston Buckie

Portsoy Macduff

Elgin Banff

A98

A96

A941 Spey Fochabers A98

A96

A95

Lossie

Keith

A97 A947 A98

Isla

Aberlour

Dufftown Huntly

Spey A95

Fiddich A941 Deveron Bogie A96

Banffshire's Courses

1 Ballindalloch Castle

2 Dufftown

3 Keith

4 Buckpool

5 Strathlene

6 Cullen

7 Duff House Royal

8 Royal Tarlair

It's
SNOWING

The Cairngorms and highlands of Banffshire provide some of the most magnificent winter wonderland scenes in Scotland. You can rarely capture in photographs the magic of God's winter but I think this chapter does the Lord justice.

*A snowbound
Ballindalloch Castle*

*The ptarmigan is an 'alpine' grouse of
the high mountain plateau, and like
the mountain hare, it changes its colour
for winter camouflage*

Winter

The snow had begun in the gloaming,
And busily all the night
Had been heaping field and highway
With a silence deep and white

James Russell Lowell, *The First Snow-Fall*

Shelterstone Crags

Ben Mheadhoin and Shelterstone Crags

Summit of Ben Macdhui in May

Walkers on the Cairngorm Plateau

When You are Lonely

When you are lonely, I wish you love.
When you are down, I wish you joy.
When you are troubled, I wish you peace.
When things are complicated, I wish you simple beauty.
When things are chaotic, I wish you inner silence.
When things look empty, I wish you hope.
I wish for both of you, a giant book imprinted on your souls
Where you shall keep all the memories you will make together.
I wish for a group of angels hovering over both of you
Every second, every minute of your lives.
I wish for both of you, happiness and the faith to see
That God blessed you both when He gave you to each other.

Anonymous

But pleasures are like poppies spread,
You seize the flow'r its bloom is shed;
Or like the snow falls in the river,
A moment white – then melts for ever.

Robert Burns, *Tam o' Shanter*

Linn Falls, Aberlour

Snow

The room was suddenly rich and the great
     bay-window was
Spawning snow and pink roses against it
Soundlessly collateral and incompatible:
World is suddener than we fancy it.

World is crazier and more of it than we think,
Incorrigibly plural. I peel and portion
A tangerine and spit the pips and feel
The drunkenness of things being various

And the fire flames with a bubbling sound
     for world
Is more spiteful and gay than one supposes –
On the tongue on the eyes on the ears
     in the palms of one's hands –
There is more than glass between the snow
     and the huge roses.

January 1953
By Louis Macneice 1907–63

Stags in a 'white out'

Skiing at the Lecht

Lecht Ski Centre 6

Cockbridge A 939
Braemar (A 93)

Ben Macdhui

Inveraven Church

Porter's Lodge, Ballindalloch

The 'Doocot', Ballindalloch

142

Cullen Auld Kirk

Aberlour Parish Church

Tomintoul, the highest village in Banffshire

The Boat Pool at Ballindalloch

St Margaret's, Aberlour

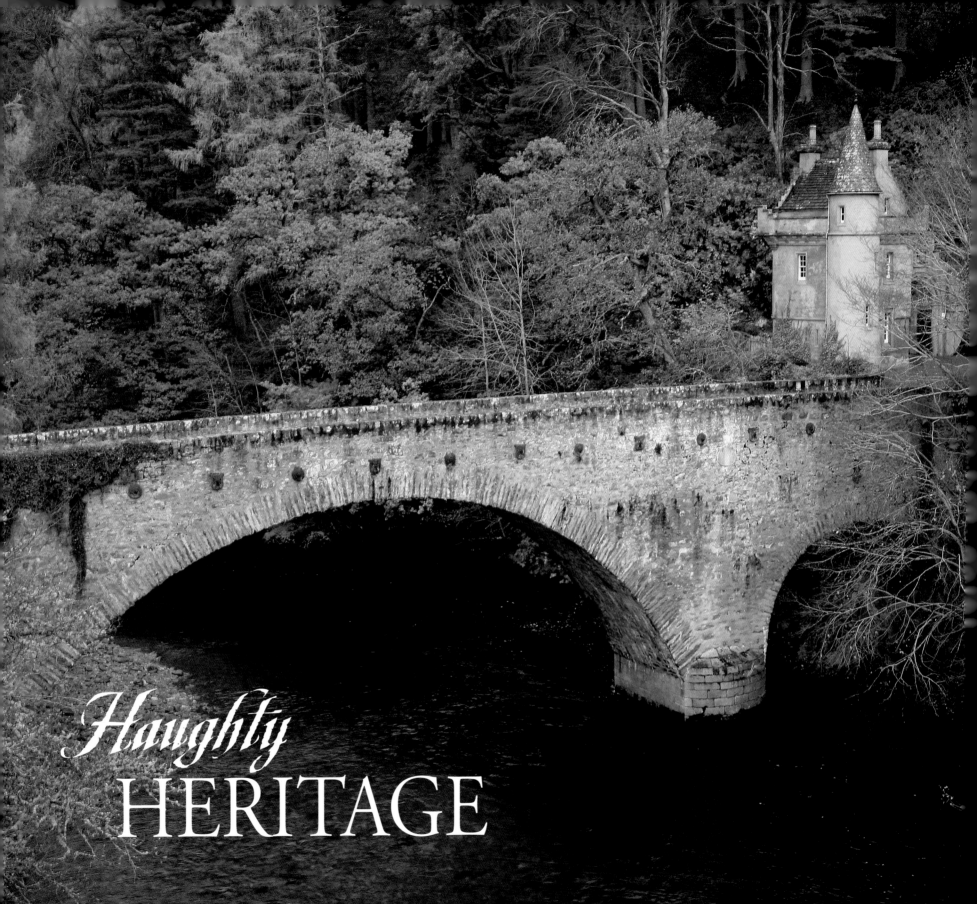

Haughty
HERITAGE

*Left: A hound gargoyle on
Ballindalloch's gatehouse*

I think probably I am fairly qualified to write a foreword to this chapter. I have spent the last 30 years of my life funding and maintaining an historic 16th-century castle. Ask the owner of any great house and they will tell you that inheriting it is the easy part; it is hanging on to it that is the hard part. Any ancient building needs constant love and attention. Banffshire is filled with hidden gems, from churches and castles to ancient bridges and historic ruins. Over the centuries, many of the castles and churches have seen clan feuding and plundering, and are now ancient ruins. Each one has its own story to tell and its own magic scenery. My home, Ballindalloch, has been lived in continuously by my family since 1546, and is one of the very few castles to still have the same family living within. This chapter is a treasure trove of magnificent architecture.

Castles & KINGS

Auchindoun Castle

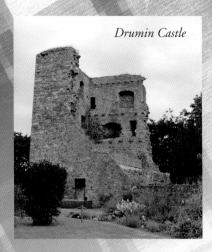
Drumin Castle

The Wolf of Badenoch (Alexander Stewart) 1342–1406

Born illegitimately to King Robert II in 1342, Alexander Stewart, the Earl of Buchan, was granted the lands of Badenoch and Strathavon in the early 1370s. His subsequent turbulent rule over the area was to earn him the name of 'Wolf of Badenoch', one of the most notorious figures in the historical landscape of northern Scotland. Cruelty, murder, rape and arson were his trademark, and never more so than following his excommunication (for deserting his wife) by the Bishop of Moray, with whom Stewart already had strained relations. Enraged by this latest slight, the Wolf embarked on a campaign of destruction along the Moray Firth coast, destroying the towns of Forres and Elgin and burning down the beautiful 'lantern of the North', Elgin Cathedral. Eventually, Stewart was forced to repent; he was pardoned by his father and even accepted back into the church. He died in 1406 (although one account puts the date earlier at 1394) and was buried at Dunkeld Cathedral where his effigy can still be seen.

Such a lifestyle required many strongholds, and Stewart's lairs included castles at Lochindorb, Loch-an-Eilein and Drumin.

Eden Castle

Cup & Saucer Windmill

Kinnairdy Castle

Findlater Castle

Boyne Castle

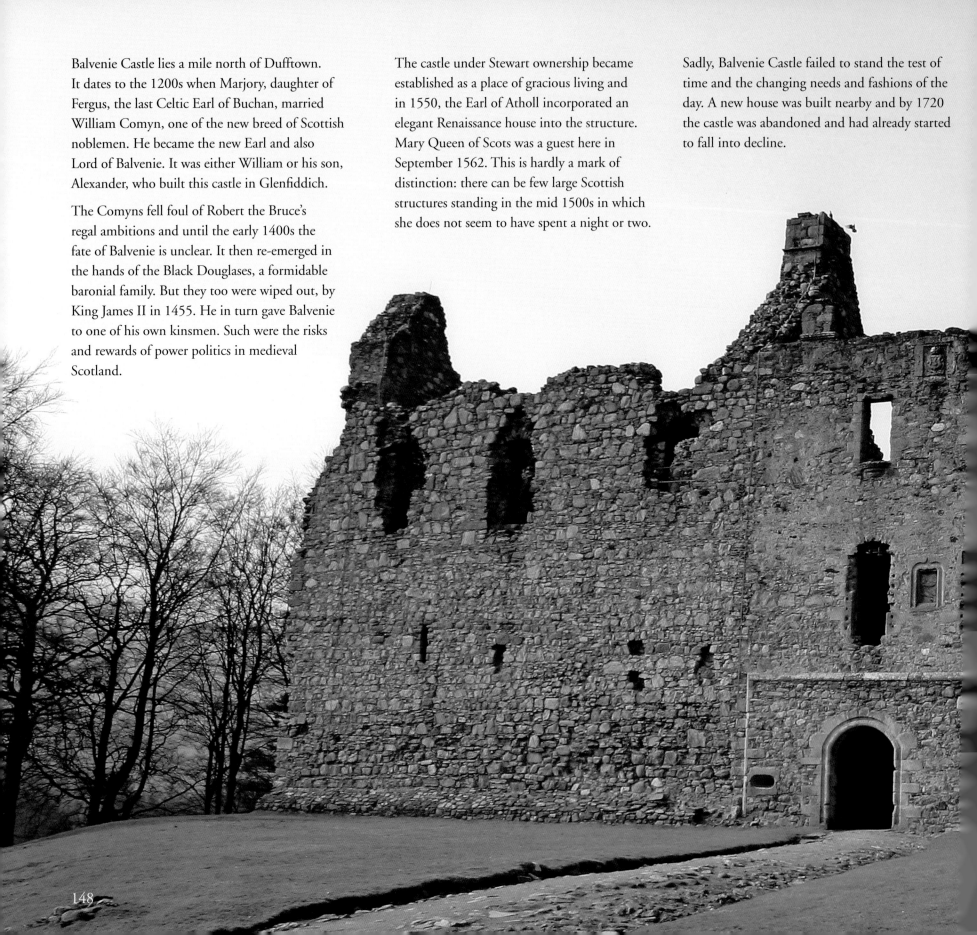

Balvenie Castle lies a mile north of Dufftown. It dates to the 1200s when Marjory, daughter of Fergus, the last Celtic Earl of Buchan, married William Comyn, one of the new breed of Scottish noblemen. He became the new Earl and also Lord of Balvenie. It was either William or his son, Alexander, who built this castle in Glenfiddich.

The Comyns fell foul of Robert the Bruce's regal ambitions and until the early 1400s the fate of Balvenie is unclear. It then re-emerged in the hands of the Black Douglases, a formidable baronial family. But they too were wiped out, by King James II in 1455. He in turn gave Balvenie to one of his own kinsmen. Such were the risks and rewards of power politics in medieval Scotland.

The castle under Stewart ownership became established as a place of gracious living and in 1550, the Earl of Atholl incorporated an elegant Renaissance house into the structure. Mary Queen of Scots was a guest here in September 1562. This is hardly a mark of distinction: there can be few large Scottish structures standing in the mid 1500s in which she does not seem to have spent a night or two.

Sadly, Balvenie Castle failed to stand the test of time and the changing needs and fashions of the day. A new house was built nearby and by 1720 the castle was abandoned and had already started to fall into decline.

Balvenie Castle

To the modern visitor Balvenie still offers a fascinating insight into life in Glenfiddich so many hundreds of years ago. And there is more remaining than you expect. Perhaps because it is so hidden by woodland, the interior is very much larger than seems possible from the outside.

Inchdrewer Castle

Milton Tower

Findochty Castle

Milton Tower (Keith)

The Tower is all that remains of the one-time Castle of Miltoun, built around 1480, home of the Royalist Ogilvie family for 200 years. An underground passage is said to run from the Auld Brig to the castle. It is said that part of the castle fell into the River Isla, and that some treasure lies in the Linn Pot, although attempts to recover it have found nothing.

'John Ogilvie of Miltoun, slain at Battle of Alford 1645, Blessed John Ogilvie, Jesuit priest martyred Glasgow Cross 1615. Castle passed by marriage to Jacobite Oliphant family 1707. Fell into ruin after 1715.'

Fortiter et Suaviter

'The blessed' John Ogilvie who was canonised by Pope Paul VI in Rome in 1976

Fordyce Castle

Ballindalloch Castle

The motto of the Macpherson Clan:
'Touch not the cat bot a glove'.
'Never meddle with a Macpherson!'

Set in the magnificent surroundings of Strathspey,
the castle is known as 'The Pearl of the North'
and is the much loved family home of the
Macpherson-Grants.
It is one of the very few privately-owned castles
to have been lived in continuously
by its original family.

Duff House

Duff House was designed by William Adam and built between 1735 and 1740 as the seat of the Earls Fife. More recently, it has been a Palm Court hotel, a sanatorium and a prisoner of war camp.

After extensive restoration in 1995, Duff House, now run by a partnership of Historic Scotland, the National Galleries of Scotland and Aberdeenshire Council, gained 5-star visitor attraction status.

Duff House organises a regular artistic programme of exhibitions, music and lectures. It is also home to a permanent collection of works of art, including chairs by Chippendale, tapestries, and old masters by artists such as Sir Henry Raeburn and El Greco.

Loveliest of trees, the cherry now

Loveliest of trees, the cherry now
Is hung with bloom along the bough,
And stands about the woodland ride
Wearing white for Eastertide.

Now, of my threescore years and ten,
Twenty will not come again,
And take from seventy springs a score,
It only leaves me fifty more.

And since to look at things in bloom
Fifty springs are little room,
About the woodlands I will go
To see the cherry hung with snow.

A.E. Housman, 1859–1936

Duff House through Banff Bridge

156

Drummuir Castle

Drummuir Castle was built in 1847 by Thomas Mackenzie for Admiral
Archibald Duff, whose distinguished career included service with Lord Nelson.

The castle is a splendid example of the Scottish Victorian architectural style.
The romantic roofline with its battlements, turrets and chimney stacks is
dominated by the 60 feet-high central lantern tower, notable for its gothic tracery.

The castle is owned by the Gordon-Duff family.

Cullen Auld Kirk & Queen Elizabeth's remains

Cullen Kirk stands on the edge of the present village, although it would have been in the middle of the main street until the early 19th century, when the whole village was moved to its present site. Records indicate that the 'interiores partes' of Queen Elizabeth de Burgh, second wife of Robert the Bruce, were buried in the church following her death in Cullen in 1327. It seems that her internal organs were removed, the better to preserve her body during its journey to Dunfermline where, as Queen, she was required to be interred. Robert the Bruce made a grant in that same year so that the chaplain of the Church would pray for the Queen's soul, and this payment has apparently been made annually, apart from one short break in the 1970s, ever since.

High on the gable end of Cullen church can be seen the remains of statuary of the Virgin Mary destroyed by marauders during the Reformation. Inside there is a marble memorial to the Earl of Findlater. The decoration on the woodwork on the Seafield family's 'pumphils' shows dates in the early 1600s, and decorative carving pre-dating this. In 1746, the church was used to stable horses by passing government troops en route to Culloden.

Cullen House

The first Lord Seafield was High Chancellor of Scotland in 1705 and was one of the Commissioners who signed the Act of Union of Scotland and England in 1707. When the Act of Union was accomplished, he gave vent to the well-known saying: 'And there's the end tae an auld sang.'

Cullen House, seat of the Seafield family

Stones & Symbols

Remembrance
by Margaret Leith Minter

In every town and village square,
we offer up a silent prayer;
for those who sleep on foreign strand,
where lonely, pristine crosses stand.
We remember them.

They left their fishing nets unwound,
their ploughs and harrows in the ground;
and marched away with heads held high,
not thinking some of them would die.
We remember them.

Father, brother, lover, son,
why were they taken one by one?
As pipers play a sad refrain,
we hear the gunfire once again.
We remember them.

With passing years, our memories fade,
but we recall the price they paid.
We still remember them.

James Ferguson, inventor and astronomer from Rothiemay

Community or family burial grounds circa 2,500 BC

Clava Cairn, Lagmore

Situated on Ballindalloch Estate, close to the confluence of the Rivers Spey and Avon, this is the only passage grave of the Clava tradition to have been identified definitely in Grampian. Four stones of the surrounding stone circle still remain erect, the tallest being 2.3m

Clava Cairn, Marionburgh

Standing on Ballindalloch Estate are five stones of a circle, the tallest stone measuring 2.74m tall. Within this circle is an inner-ring cairn comprising a circular bank of small stones.

General Wade and his bridges

General George Wade was appointed Commander-in-Chief Northern Britain in 1725 and began a programme of road-building by the military that revolutionised communications in the north of Scotland. Although the purpose of so doing was actually to improve the road network so that Government forces could move more swiftly to pacify rebellious clans (thus hastening the demise of the clan system) the resulting road improvements were much to the benefit of the country in the long run, giving rise to the saying:

> *'If you'd seen these roads before they were made*
> *You'd lift up your arms and bless General Wade'.*

Ironically, these lines were apparently penned by Wade's successor, General Caulfeild who, after Wade's retirement in 1740, actually oversaw the building of many more miles of road than Wade had done! One of the roads made under Caulfeild was the Lecht, on the present A939. Beside a spring at the Well of the Lecht, a rough-cut slab left by the builders of the military road reads:

> *AD 1754*
>
> *Five Companies The 33rd Regiment*
> *Right Honbl Lord Chas. Hay Colonel*
> *Made the road from here to the Spey*

Top: The Wade bridge over the Avon, near Tomintoul, provided the main route across the river for many centuries until wear and tear took its toll. It was replaced in 1991 with a new bridge upstream
Above: The other Wade bridge in the county is at the Porter's Lodge, Ballindalloch, again over the River Avon

Packhorse Bridge at Glenlivet

Banff Castle

The Roman Catholic Chapel, Banff

Churches & Memorials

Banff Parish Church

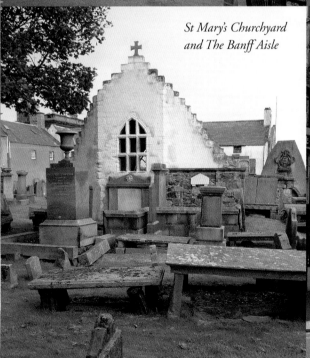
St Mary's Churchyard and The Banff Aisle

Biggar Fountain, Banff

St Andrew's Episcopal Church, Banff

This imposing structure
was constructed to John
Fowlie's design by two
experienced masons,
Alexander Brown and
Magnus Johnstone,
between April 1921
and October 1922.
It is 70 feet high
with a base
diameter of
18 feet.

War Memorial at Macduff

*Jubilee Fountain,
Aberchirder*

*18th-century ship's anchor,
Macduff*

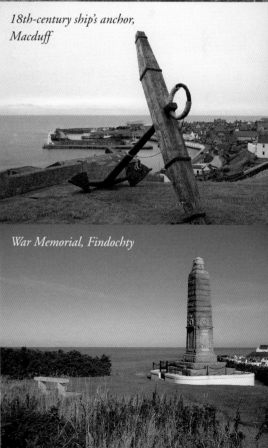

War Memorial, Findochty

165

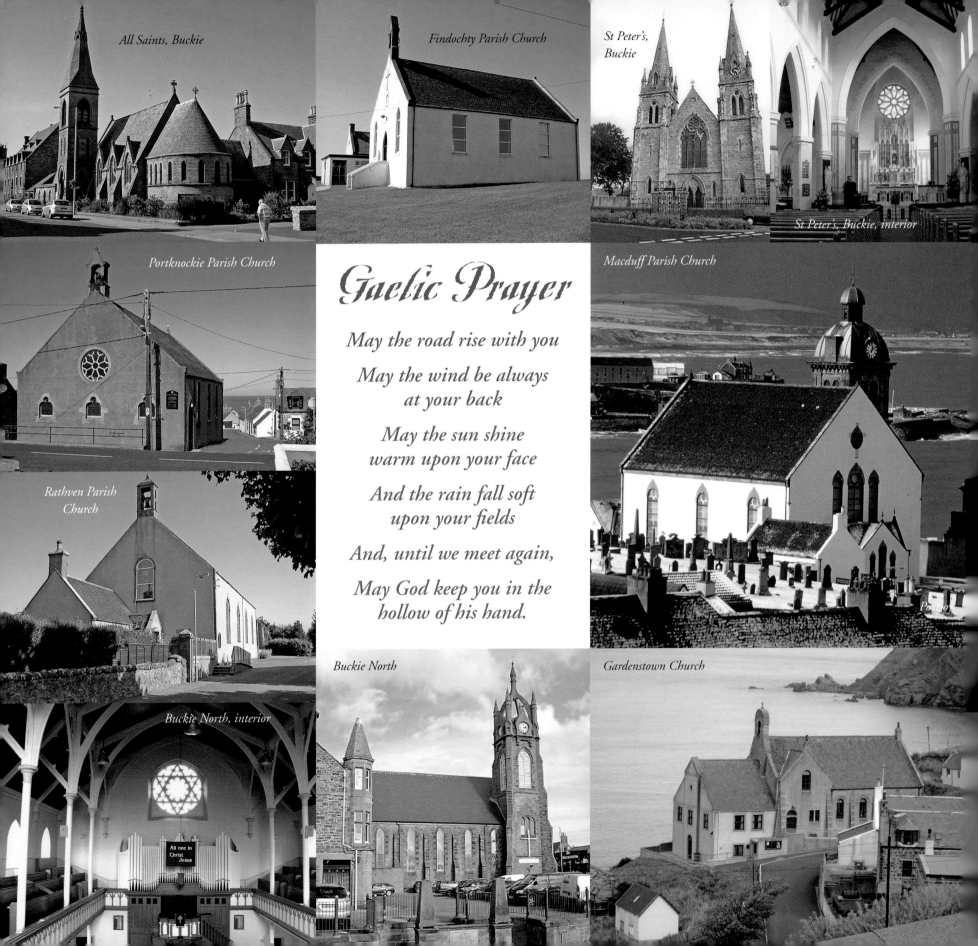

All Saints, Buckie

Findochty Parish Church

St Peter's, Buckie

St Peter's, Buckie, interior

Portknockie Parish Church

Macduff Parish Church

Rathven Parish Church

Portsoy

Gaelic Prayer

May the road rise with you

May the wind be always
at your back

May the sun shine
warm upon your face

And the rain fall soft
upon your fields

And, until we meet again,

May God keep you in the
hollow of his hand.

Buckie North, interior

Buckie North

Gardenstown Church

All one in
Christ Jesus

St Rufus, Keith

Mortlach Parish Church, Dufftown

Craigellachie Church

North Kirk, Keith

St Thomas, Keith

Cornhill Parish Church

Fordyce Church, Portsoy

Marnoch Old Church, Aberchirder

First Free Church in Scotland, New Marnoch Church, Aberchirder

St Marnan Episcopal Church, Aberchirder

St Michael's, Tomintoul

Marnoch Church & the Disruption

Marnoch Kirk was built in 1792 to replace an old church in the cemetery beside the river Deveron; it is on the site of an old stone circle.

The ministers at that time were appointed by the patrons (in Marnoch's case, the Earl of Fife), but in 1837 the popular minister the Rev. William Stronach died, and the patrons appointed a Mr Edwards, who was not at all to the congregation's liking. There ensued, for several years, a locally divisive and legal struggle, which was mirrored in other parishes in Scotland.

This came to a climax on Sunday 3rd January 1841 when the most part of Marnoch's congregation walked out of the kirk into the snow and worshipped in temporary accommodation by the river.

They immediately began to raise funds for a new church and manse to be built in Aberchirder. Hardly a year later, on 17th March 1842, the handsome new church was opened as the first Free Church in Scotland.

This and other events throughout Scotland led to the formation of the Free Church of Scotland in May 1843, when some 450 ministers left the established Church of Scotland; this exodus is commonly known as the Disruption.

In 1953 the two Marnoch congregations and their churches were reunited to become the new Church of Marnoch under the Church of Scotland.

Scalan, the hidden college in the Braes of Glenlivet where Roman Catholic priests were trained in secret during the 18th century

Famous PEOPLE *and* QUIRKY *Stories*

I think the heading speaks for itself. These are some of the famous and infamous characters of Banffshire which make its history.

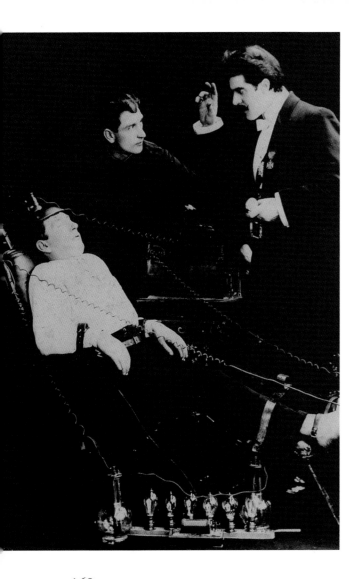

Walford Bodie

Samuel Murphy Bodie, born in Aberdeen in 1869, was to become one of Scotland's best-known and most flamboyant entertainers. Bodie settled in Macduff after his marriage to a local girl, Jeannie Henry, and later, in 1906, built the handsome Manor House on Skene Street. He also took a keen interest in the town, building a public swimming pool and baths for the townfolk, and officially opening the Royal Tarlair Golf Course in 1926.

However, 'Dr Walford Bodie MD', as he styled himself, was also a master showman, amazing the audiences of the time with magic, hypnotism, ventriloquism and electrical experiments. Capitalising on public horror at the first execution in the electric chair, Bodie proceeded to build a replica and terrified his audiences with fake electrocutions. (In 1920, he was presented with the original chair from Sing Sing prison by his friend, Harry Houdini.)

There soon arose public suspicion about his performances, and objections to his use of the letters MD, which Bodie claimed stood for 'Merry Devil' – he was forced to leave the stage at the Glasgow Coliseum by medical students who pelted him with 'ochre, peasemeal, eggs and decayed herrings'. However, the continued publicity meant he still had an audience, and he continued to perform, dying, at the age of 70, at the end of a season at the Blackpool Pleasure Beach.

Bodie's first wife, Jeannie, died in 1931 and not long after, he married a young dancer named Florrie Robertshaw. Bodie also outlived two of his children: 'Bodie's Fountain' was erected a few hundred yards from the Manor House in memory of his daughter, Jeannie, who died in 1909 at the age of 19; and his eldest son, Albert, died in 1915 aged 26 years.

Macpherson's Rant (Lament)

One of the most famous of Scottish outlaws, James Macpherson was reputed to be the son of a Highland laird, Macpherson of Invereshie (a relation of the author, Clare Macpherson-Grant Russell) and a gypsy girl. James was brought up in his father's house, but after Invereshie's death – he was killed as he attempted to recover cattle taken by reivers – he was reclaimed by the gypsy band.

An accomplished swordsman and fiddler, James became the leader of the gypsies. He appears to have been a Scottish 'Robin Hood', terrorising to some extent the rich landowners and farmers of the north-east, but he was eventually betrayed by a member of his own tribe. He escaped and was recaptured several times before his trial took place, his final attempt to run being foiled by a woman who dropped a blanket over his head. He was eventually brought to trial at Banff on 8th November 1700, accused, amongst other things, of being an 'Egyptian' or gypsy, which was a capital offence in Scotland at that time.

Whilst under sentence of death, Macpherson is said to have composed the famous 'Macpherson's Rant', which he played on the

gallows before breaking the fiddle over his knee so that no other could play it.

Legend has it that a reprieve was on its way to Banff at the time of the execution, but the authorities, seeing a lone rider approaching and assuming, correctly, that he carried a pardon for James Macpherson, turned the hands of the town clock forward by 15 minutes and hanged him before the pardon could arrive:

The reprieve, it was comin o'er the Brig o' Banff
Tae set Macpherson free
But they set the clock a quarter afore
And they hanged him tae the tree

'The Monocled Mutineer'

On 1st June 1920, a remote cottage near Tomintoul was the unlikely setting for two attempted murders, part of the strange story of Percy Toplis, the 'Monocled Mutineer'.

Born in Derbyshire in 1896, Toplis, a thief and trickster, even as a boy, had committed a string of criminal offences before he enlisted in the army in 1914, serving in Gallipoli, Greece, Egypt, Mesopotamia and India. He apparently deserted and re-joined the army several times, and combined his military career with fraud and racketeering.

Wanted in connection with the murder of a taxi driver near Andover in April 1920, Toplis, a talented impersonator, deserted again and spent some time masquerading among London society as an army officer, complete with trademark monocle and loaded gun. As the search for him intensified, Toplis fled to Scotland, seeking anonymity in a remote bothy at the foot of the Lecht, where it seems that he lived undetected until a cold snap forced him to light a fire in the bothy for warmth. On 1st June, a local farmer saw smoke issuing from the chimney, became suspicious and approached the cottage, along with a gamekeeper and the local policeman. After a short conversation Toplis, without warning, produced his revolver and fired at the visitors, wounding the farmer and the policeman. He then cycled off towards Aberdeen, leaving an unpaid bicycle repair bill in Tomintoul.

Toplis abandoned the bicycle in Aberdeen and headed south by train, pausing in Edinburgh to pawn his watch, before continuing to Cumbria where he sought, and received, accommodation and refreshment from the army at Carlisle Castle!

On 6th June, a local policeman questioned a man in military dress sitting at the roadside near Penrith. Unsatisfied with the man's response, the policeman made some further checks and, now convinced that he had found the man wanted for the Andover murder, returned with reinforcements and confronted Toplis, who was subsequently shot and fatally wounded.

The name of 'Monocled Mutineer' has been attached to Toplis since his story was published in a book of that name, and refers to his supposed heroic part in a six-day mutiny which broke out among British troops in an army camp in France in 1917. As with so many other aspects of Percy Toplis' life, it is not clear whether this was fact or fiction.

James Ferguson, 1710–1776

Self-taught Rothiemay man, James Ferguson, former shepherd, miller, doctor's assistant, portrait-painter, inventor and astronomer – elected Fellow of the Royal Society of London.

James Ferguson was a Scottish astronomer and instrument-maker, born near Rothiemay in Banffshire of parents in very humble circumstances. He first learned to read by overhearing his father teach his elder brother, and with the help of an old woman was able, he says in his autobiography, to read tolerably well before his father thought of teaching him. After receiving further instruction in reading from his father, who also taught him to write, he was sent at the age of seven for three months to the grammar school at Keith. His taste for mechanics was about this time accidentally awakened on seeing his father making use of a lever to raise a part of the roof of his house — an exhibition of seeming strength which at first excited his terror as well as wonder. In 1720 he was sent to a neighbouring farm to keep sheep, where in the daytime he amused himself by making models of mills and other machines, and at night in studying the stars. Afterwards, as a servant with a miller, and then with a doctor, he met with hardships which rendered his constitution feeble through life. Being compelled by his weak health to return home, he there amused himself by making a clock with wooden wheels and a whalebone spring. When slightly recovered he showed this and some other inventions to a neighbouring gentleman, who engaged him to clean his clocks, and also desired him to make his house his home. He there began to draw patterns for needlework, and his success in this art led him to think of becoming a painter.

River Deveron at Rothiemay

In 1734 he went to Edinburgh, where he began to take portraits in miniature, by which means, while engaged in his scientific studies, he supported himself and his family for many years. Subsequently he settled at Inverness, where he drew up his Astronomical Rotula for showing the motions of the planets, places of the sun and moon, etc., and in 1743 went to London, England, which was his home for the rest of his life. He wrote various papers for the Royal Society of London, of which he became a fellow in 1763, devised astronomical and mechanical models, and in 1748 began to give public lectures on experimental philosophy. These he repeated in most of the principal towns in England. His deep interest in his subject, his clear explanations, his ingeniously constructed diagrams, and his mechanical apparatus rendered him one of the most successful of popular lecturers on scientific subjects. It is, however, as the inventor and improver of astronomical and other scientific apparatus, and as a striking instance of self-education, that he claims a place among the most remarkable men of science of his country. During the latter years of his life he was in receipt of a pension of £50 from the privy purse. He died in London on 17th November 1776.

Charlie 'The Hermit' Marioni

In 1920, Charlie Marioni built himself a lean-to shelter against the rocks at Sunnyside Bay, east of Cullen. He stayed there alone for 13 years, lived off the sea, snared rabbits, and grew and sold vegetables from the raised beds he built in front of his home. He is believed to have been a sailor from the French navy who failed to return to his ship after shore leave. In 1933 he was eventually summoned to appear before the Sheriff at Banff as an alien and ordered to register. He refused, and was fined 20 shillings; then the Magistrate shook his hand and wished him 'good luck'. Charlie left, and disappeared.

Charlie's badly overgrown stone-edged vegetable beds are all that remain to prove his existence.

James Gordon Bennett

James Gordon Bennett was born in 1792 in Enzie. Soon afterwards his parents moved to Newmill, where he was reared and educated at a school in Newmill and at Keith Public School. In 1819 he emigrated to America and drifted into a variety of jobs. Finally he entered the newspaper business and in 1835 he published the first copy of the 'New York Herald'. It was an instant success and made James Gordon Bennett a millionaire. He died in New York in 1872. His son, also named James Gordon Bennett, was born in 1841 in America. James and his sister, however, were educated in Paris.

When James Jnr became an adult he returned to work with his father in the 'New York Herald' office. James Jnr, however, preferred a European lifestyle and moved back to Paris where he established the 'International Herald Tribune'. On his father's death, he inherited both newspaper empires. He did not neglect his inheritance. 'The New York Herald' continued to thrive and he laid a new Transatlantic cable so he could contact his newspaper from Europe. He also funded an Arctic expedition and sent Stanley Morton to find the explorer David Livingstone. He sponsored a number of sports, particularly those requiring impressive and expensive equipment, including motor racing, motorcycle racing, ballooning and air-racing. He died and was buried in Paris 1918. The expression 'Gordon Bennett' came about because of the outrageous lifestyle of James Jnr and is still used as an expletive for shock or surprise.

William Boyd, 1885–1979

This Scottish Canadian pathologist, academic and author, was known for his medical textbooks. Born locally in Portsoy, he received his medical degree at the University of Edinburgh and went on to become Professor of Pathology in Manitoba, Canada. He was made Companion of the Order of Canada, the country's highest civilian honour.

The 'Girl Pat'

This most unusual incident took place a few years before WWII. Grimsby was the main fishing port in the world, and the 'Girl Pat' was a 75-foot motor fishing vessel, used for short fishing trips in the North Sea.

The Skipper 'Dod' Osborne of Buckie, with his crew of six, had not landed any record catches. As a result there was a strong rumour that the vessel owners were planning to take her out of commission as she was not paying her way, so the skipper came up with a plan. They would leave on a fishing trip in the normal way, but would sail southwards, into the English Channel, then south through the Bay of Biscay, across the Atlantic to South America where they could make a living using 'Girl Pat' for ferrying cargo. Ridiculous and preposterous, but the more they thought about it, the more they fancied the idea. They knew they had five days before the theft of the vessel came to light, so they sailed south but had to call in at Dover because one of the crew was taken ill, and a temporary engineer did not go along with the idea. They landed them both, and set off immediately on the next leg which took them to Dakar, West Africa.

Although the theft had now come to light, the news was confined to the UK, so they were able to dock at Dakar, re-fuel, take on provisions (all at the owners' expense) and set sail for their next port of call, the Azores. Unfortunately, with their limited navigation equipment (a school atlas!), they missed it completely, and after seven or eight days sailing westwards, were nearly out of food and water. In an attempt to conserve fuel they rigged a jury sail and, when the wind was favourable, were able to make two or three knots under sail. They sighted a passenger liner, and showed a distress flare, causing the liner to heave to. But by this time the name 'Girl Pat' had become world news, and although they had removed the name from the bows the captain of the liner realised who they were, did not give them food, and left them to it, after notifying the authorities of their position. They eventually reached Georgetown and all were arrested and brought back to the UK.

On 19th October 1937, they appeared at the Old Bailey charged with theft and Skipper Osborne was sentenced to 18 months Hard Labour. The public were fascinated by the saga of the 'Girl Pat', but many locals were hugely critical of Osborne for abandoning his family. As a conseqence, Osborne did not return to Grimsby after his release; he made a living by giving talks about his adventures and visited the United States hoping he would be received better, but he never made a fortune. When the war started, he joined the Royal Navy. He would normally have been commissioned as a Skipper RNR with his Board of Trade Certificate of Competency, but his conviction prevented this – although he did reach the rank of Chief Petty Officer, and spent his war years as Coxswain on a drifter at Belfast, used as an examination vessel.

Although there were many rumours about his war-time service, they were myths established by one of his crew who was with him on the drifter. After the war, things did not go too well with him. He tried to cash in on his name and the 'Girl Pat' but was not very successful and eventually committed suicide in a small hotel room in Paris.

But what of the 'Girl Pat'? She was brought back to this country and, due to her fame, was put on show at Blackpool and other resorts. In the couple of years before war started, she made far more money for her owners by this than she ever did when she was fishing.

When Dod and the 'Girl Pat' were a celebrity tourist attraction postcards of the vessel with his portrait were distributed widely. This one was actually sent by Dod Osborne himself to his daughter

Richard Gordon of Banff

Richard Alexander Stuart Gordon (b. 1947) is a Scottish author born in Banff, who has written numerous science fiction novels, encyclopedias, and travel guides. Gordon's novels are noted for their mix of historical fact and creative fictionalised events.

Due to objections from publishers to his using his given name because there was already a published Richard Gordon, Gordon published many of his best-known works under the pen names Alex R. Stuart and Stuart Gordon.

One interesting note of Gordon's work is the colourful dedications in his earliest works, such as the *The Bikers*: To She Who Types Like a Drunken Midget Playing The Piano.

While Gordon has never written fictional pieces set in Scotland, the characters in his books occasionally pass through his hometown. In *Fire in the Abyss,* time-warped Sir Humphrey Gilbert passes through Buckie, where Gordon grew up. Gordon is currently teaching in China.

Three spies at Portgordon!

In 1940, three Nazi spies landed from the sea near Portgordon. The vigilance of the station master, the porter and policemen resulted in their capture. After trial, two men were hanged and a woman imprisoned.

James Sinclair of Banff

James Sinclair, PC (26th May 1908– 7th February 1984) was a Canadian politician and businessman.

Born in Banff, he moved to Vancouver with his family in 1911. He studied engineering at the University of British Columbia and was awarded a Rhodes scholarship in 1928 to study mathematics at the University of Oxford. He also studied mathematical physics at Princeton University. During World War II, he served with the Royal Canadian Air Force in North Africa, Malta, and Sicily.

He was first elected to the Canadian House of Commons representing the riding of Vancouver North in the 1940 federal election, and was the only MP who served in WWII. A Liberal, he was re-elected in 1945, 1949, 1953, and 1957. He was defeated in the 1958 federal election. From 1949 to 1952, he was the Parliamentary Assistant to the Minister of Finance. From 1952 to 1957, he was the Minister of Fisheries.

From 1958 to 1960, he was the President of the Fisheries Association of British Columbia. From 1960 to 1970, he was President and Chairman of Lafarge Cement of North America. From 1970 to 1973, he was Deputy Chairman of Canada Cement Lafarge Limited.

He is the father of Margaret Sinclair, one-time wife of Prime Minister Pierre Trudeau.

Captain George Duff & Norwich Duff – Heroes of Trafalgar

Born in Banff in 1764, son of the Banff Sheriff Clerk of the time and great-nephew of the first Earl of Fife, George Duff had a passion for the sea which obviously ran in the family's blood. At the age of 13 he joined his great-uncle, Captain Robert Duff (later to become Vice Admiral), in the Mediterranean. George Duff's capabilities ensured his swift promotion, and he had seen action on both sides of the Atlantic before being given command of HMS *Mars,* aboard which he lost his life during the Battle of Trafalgar in 1805. His 13-year-old son, Norwich Duff, who was also aboard *Mars,* had the sad duty of writing to inform his mother of his father's death. Norwich Duff went on to have a distinguished naval career himself, gaining the rank of Vice Admiral in 1857.

William Gordon Stables — the First Caravaner

William Gordon Stables MD, CM. RN was born in Aberchirder, in Banffshire, on 21st May 1840. After studying medicine at the University of Aberdeen, he served as a surgeon in the Royal Navy. He came ashore in 1875, and settled in Twyford, Berkshire, in England.

He wrote over 130 books. The bulk of his large output is boys' adventure fiction, often with a nautical or historical setting. He also wrote books on health, fitness and medical subjects, and the keeping of cats and dogs. He was a copious contributor of articles and stories to the *Boy's Own Paper*.

He is also notable as the first person to order a "gentleman's caravan" from the Bristol Carriage Company, in which he travelled the length of Great Britain in 1885 (the subject of his book *The Gentleman Gypsy*).

He died in Twyford on 10th May 1910.

Bridge of Alvah on the River Deveron

Stanley Bruce — The Bard of Banff

Duff House
A Walk from Duff House to the Bridge of Alvah

Departing from Duff House,
in the spot where the Earls of Fife once stood,
we'll wander through the Fife gates
and into 'Wrack Wood'.

Not far along the track,
an old 'Ice House' you can see,
it was Duff House's refrigerator,
but now it's history.

A little bit further,
a 'Mausoleum' you will find,
built by the 2nd Earl in 1790,
and has an old monument behind.

This Gothic style building,
was originally built with no wood,
it used to have stained glass windows,
and elegantly it stood.

But the original roof did leak
and in the 19th Century they did tile,
but it's still a wonderful building,
with character and style.

The Burial vault is underground,
21 coffins it does contain,
including the 1st Earl and the Countess,
who the 2nd Earl brought home.

Two miles away,
is the most beautiful scenic spot,
it's called the 'Bridge of Alvah'
and I'm sure you'll like it a lot!

This single arched bridge,
was built in 1772,
it stands about 40 feet high,
a crossing over the Deveron for you.

On the other side,
is the 'Montcoffer Wood',
you can follow the track further,
to Macduff if you're in the mood.

Stanley Bruce. 8th January 2004

175

Lord Byron AND *Banffshire*

She Walks In Beauty

She walks in beauty, like the night
Of cloudless climes and starry skies;
And all that's best of dark and bright
Meet in her aspect and her eyes:
Thus mellow'd to that tender light
Which heaven to gaudy day denies.

One shade the more, one ray the less,
Had half impair'd the nameless grace
Which waves in every raven tress,
Or softly lightens o'er her face;
Where thoughts serenely sweet express
How pure, how dear their dwelling-place.

And on that cheek, and o'er that brow,
So soft, so calm, yet eloquent,
The smiles that win, the tints that glow,
But tell of days in goodness spent,
A mind at peace with all below,
A heart whose love is innocent!

Lord Byron

Banffshire is also 'spiritual' home to one of literature's most colourful and flamboyant characters, George Gordon Byron, later Lord Byron; Romantic Poet.

Born in humble circumstances in London in 1788, he and his Scottish mother, Catherine Gordon of Gight, from Banffshire, moved back to Scotland a year later in 1789, and for the next nine years of his life, the troublesome and precocious lad was brought up a Scot. As he said later, 'born half a Scot and bred a whole one'.

Attending Aberdeen Grammar School – where there is a statue of Byron today – he would accompany his mother on regular visits to relations such as her grandmother, Margaret Duff Gordon, Lady Gight, at Banff. It was here that he dressed a pillow up as himself and threw it out of an upstairs window, much to the consternation of outraged relatives below!

In 1798, Byron's uncle, The Wicked Lord, died, and the 10-year-old became Lord Byron, taking up his inheritance of Newstead Abbey in Nottinghamshire. The rest, as they say, is history.

Although he travelled widely throughout Britain and Europe he never returned to Scotland, but sought out the company of Scotsmen wherever he went. Fellow writer, Walter Scott was a great admirer and friend, and Byron's poetry is full of references to Scotland, its way of life, its climate and culture. Towards the end of his life in Italy and finally in Greece, he was so proud of his Scottish ancestry that virtually his whole wardrobe was created from Gordon tartan and other closely related plaids.

An interpretation showing Byron as a boy, with his first love, Mary Duff.

My heart warms to the Tartan

The Romantic Poet, Byron, died a hero in Greece in 1824. To his dying day he never forgot his Scottish roots. In this evocation of his last days, he wears a pelisse of Gordon Tartan.

Watercolour by Nick McCann, courtesy of Geoffrey Bond, OBE

General Grant

General James Grant was no ordinary soldier. Destined, as the second son of the house, to serve in the army, James Grant entered military service as a young man and retired from it after 60 years continuous service. During this time he rose from impoverished army officer to Governor of Florida, a position which he was awarded in recognition of his distinguished service in the Seven Years War (1756–63) which raged throughout the colonies.

The General's shrewd development of an indigo plantation proved highly successful and, upon inheriting Ballindalloch Castle from his brother in 1770, he was able to use his assets to add new north and south wings to the house.

He rejoined the colours on the outbreak of the American War of Independence, consolidating his reputation as a *bon viveur* whilst there by dining off porcelain and silver in his tent, even as the bullets flew outside.

His investments continued to flourish, and General Grant was a wealthy man when he returned again to Ballindalloch Castle, where the improvements he made included the building of a wing to house his favourite chef, a French-speaking African slave.

General Grant's fondness for the good life gave rise to the belief that he was the fattest man in Scotland when he died in 1806, but his outstanding legacy was the financial security he brought to Ballindalloch for generations to come.

The coat of arms of the Macpherson-Grant family

General James Grant by 18th-century Scottish Society portraitist, Allan Ramsay

The CANADIAN CONNECTION

Lord Mount Stephen

George Stephen was born in Dufftown in 1829, the son of a carpenter. He was educated at the local school, then began his working life on a farm before emigrating to Canada at the age of 21 to work in a relative's textile business. An astute businessman, he was running his own wool-importing company by 1866, as well as beginning to invest in other enterprises, including the railroad business. Stephen's financial acumen led to his eventual appointment as President of the Bank of Montreal, and then to his company's winning of a contract to build the Canadian Pacific Railway. Despite many hurdles and setbacks, Stephen succeeded in putting together the complicated financial structure required to complete the massive project. He retired, a very wealthy man, to England where he was created Baron Mount Stephen in 1891.

George Stephen, born 5th June 1829, in Dufftown
Banffshire. Died 29th November 1921, aged 92

181

Driving the last spike, 7th November 1885

Railway section men (workers), Beaver River Canyon, BC c.1885)

First train at Port Moody, BC, 4th July 1886

Dining Car 'Holyrood', c.1885

Canadian Pacific Railway

The completion of a transcontinental railway within 10 years was a condition of British Columbia's entry into the Confederation. After much bitter competition to secure the lucrative contract, interests led by George Stephen, originally from Banffshire, and Donald A. Smith finally triumphed, and the Canadian Pacific Railway was incorporated on 16th February 1881.

The demand for early completion, coupled with the immense difficulties in construction, ensured that the CPR received generous provisions, including $25 million in cash and huge tracts of land alongside the railway.

Construction proceeded rapidly across the plains. However, as the rail line reached the Rocky Mountains, thousands of men were required for the labour-intensive tasks of building bridges, erecting snow sheds and blasting tunnels through the most difficult terrain of all. Nevertheless, the transcontinental rail line was completed five-and-a-half years ahead of schedule.

The line through to the Pacific coast was completed in 1885, and marked by the driving of the 'Last Spike' at Craigellachie in Eagle Pass on 7th November of that year; the first through passenger train left Montreal on 28th June 1886, arriving at Port Moody in British Columbia on 4th July.

The Banffshire sleeping car

The Banffshire

The Banffshire sleeping car has an interesting history. It began service in 1926, when it boasted 14 seating sections which were convertible into 14 sets of upper and lower berths, a men's smoking room and washroom, a ladies' lounge and washroom, a kitchen and a linen closet. In 1937, air conditioning was added – huge underslung bunkers carried some 4,500 lbs of ice, of which 300 lbs an hour was needed to keep passengers comfortable.

The car was upgraded and modernised again in 1951, and re-named *Golden*. Between subsequent periods of disuse, it served on the special steam train that pulled dignitaries to the re-enactment of the driving of the last spike at Craigellachie, BC, on the 100th anniversary, 7th November 1985, of the original event.

When the Canadian Pacific Railway needed a dedicated, first-class stateroom car for its newly-launched Royal Canadian Pacific luxury cruise train, the *Golden* was selected for a million-dollar heritage retro-refurbishment, but with modern air conditioning, washroom and shower facilities for each stateroom. In 2003 the car was launched as the *Banffshire* – named after the county where George Stephen, co-founder and first president of CPR, was born.

The ROYAL SCOTSMAN

Originally launched in May 1985, the train, in its current form, dates from May 1990. The owners put together a set of carriages (all rather different), which were rented in and called The Royal Scotsman, launching in the spring of 1985. The carriage leases ran for five years and it was a success – the train won the Queen's Award for Export.

After the initial five-year period elapsed, the decision was taken to purchase outright a different set of carriages, designed to the owners' specifications. Working with designer James Park, 10 Pullman carriages were subsequently bought and transformed with all the interior woodwork made to specification by a specialist woodworking company in Bournemouth and shipped to the construction site and installed. This second rake of carriages replaced the first in May 1990. The new rake incorporated many improvements – each cabin now had its own private facilities, steam heating was replaced by electric heating, there was seating for all at the same time in the Observation and Dining Cars and capacity moved from 28 to 32. In 1997, the capacity was further increased from 32 to 36 to provide 16 twin and four single state cabins.

The quintessential Royal Scotsman experience is certainly one of the most popular journeys. After following the east coast up to Keith it heads across to the picturesque west coast village of Plockton – where the cult classic, The Wicker Man, *was filmed* – before making its way to Inverness and then south to Perth. The train then visits Strathisla and Ballindalloch, with its magnificent castle and gardens; home of Oliver and Clare Russell and their family. The journey has opportunities for fishing, clay pigeon shooting or guided walking along Caledonian pine forest trails.

Ballindalloch Castle, home of
Oliver and Clare Russell

Owned by Orient-Express Hotels, Trains & Cruises and operated by The Great Scottish & Western Railway Company, today's Royal Scotsman set is thus the second to carry its name. The running order of The Royal Scotsman carriages is: Observation Car with verandah viewing platform; Dining Car Number One (Raven); Dining Car Number Two (Victory); State Car number one, two, three, four and five; and a Service Car. The sequence is in running order from the rear so guests can best enjoy the passing countryside.

At one end of the train is perhaps the most distinctive vehicle, the open-ended Observation Car, converted from the Pullman kitchen car, Snipe. Originally built in 1960 by the Metropolitan-Cammell Carriage and Wagon Company, it entered service in 1961 as a First Class kitchen car. In 1989, the car was bought from its private owner, Michael Bailiss, and converted to its current luxury configuration, able to comfortably hold all 36 guests at any time.

Adjacent to this is Dining Car Number One, which is still referred to by its former Pullman car name, Raven. Colin Angell, a firm of cabinet makers from Evesham, Worcestershire, won the contract to transform a 1962 second-class Pullman carriage into Raven, with a capacity for 20 guests.

Next in the formation is Dining Car Number Two, known as Victory and so-called since it was built in 1945. Victory was built as a London & North Eastern Railway Director's Saloon and acquired from Sir Bill McAlpine. The transformation was completed in a number of weeks – from its bright orange curtains and brushed aluminium fittings to wood-panelling, inlaid with intricate marquetry, mahogany veneer cupboards and specially-made dining chairs and tables – not to mention a state-of-the-art modern kitchen. Eight marquetry panels with intricate designs of thistles, flowing ribbons and butterflies line the walls and an inlaid frieze of several different woods runs on into the corridors. Victory can accommodate up to 16 guests, ensuring all guests can dine at the same sitting across the two dining cars.

The five State Sleeping Cars follow. These cars, like the Verandah car, were originally built as Pullman Cars in 1960 by the Metropolitan-Cammell Carriage and Wagon Company.

The Sleeping Cars provide 16 twin cabins and four single State Cabins, beautifully fitted out in rich marquetry. All cabins have fixed lower beds, dressing table, full-length wardrobe, individually controlled heating, cooling ceiling fans, opening windows and cabin service call button. Each cabin has its own private facilities with shower, wash-basin and toilet and a constant supply of hot water.

The Royal Scotsman's routes take in some of Scotland's most romantic and iconic sights and landmarks, such as the Forth and Tay bridges; to be enjoyed from the luxurious interiors of the train

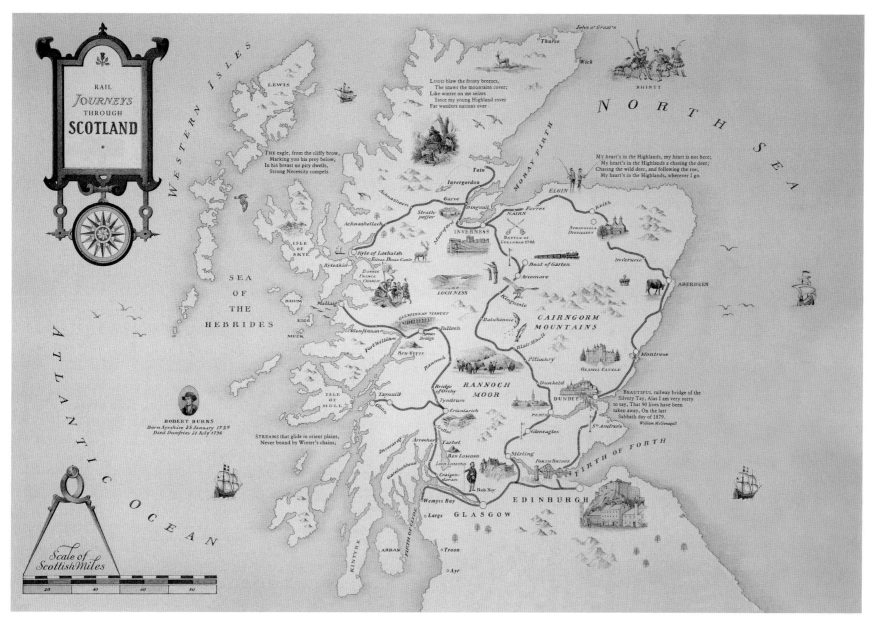

New *CHALLENGES*

In the last decade concern about global warming has brought the search for renewable energy to the forefront of government policy.

A small number of potential onshore windfarm sites had been identified in local government long-term plans and private sector developers did their own research on these and other sites.

Following an extensive planning process, windfarms in Banffshire are now operational at Boyndie Airfield and Paul's Hill on Ballindalloch Estate.

O Caledonia! stern and wild,
Meet nurse for a poetic child!
Land of brown heath and shaggy wood,
Land of the mountain and the flood,
Land of my sires! what mortal hand
Can e'er untie the filial band
That knits me to thy rugged strand!

Sir Walter Scott, *The Lay of the Last Minstrel*

Deep peace of the running wave to you
Deep peace of the flowing air to you
Deep peace of the quiet earth to you
Deep peace of the shining stars to you
Deep peace of the Son of peace to you

Sunsets

Silver

Slowly, silently, now the moon
Walks the night in her silver shoon;
This way, and that, she peers, and sees
Silver fruit upon silver trees;
One by one the casements catch
Her beams beneath the silvery thatch;
Crouched in his kennel, like a log,
With paws of silver sleeps the dog;
From their shadowy cote the white breasts peep
Of doves in a silver-feathered sleep;
A harvest mouse goes scampering by,
With silver claws, and silver eye;
And moveless fish in the water gleam,
By silver reeds in a silver stream.

Walter de la Mare 1873–1956

194

The Heavenly Dancers

Whisht whisht
Look up to the sky
See the heavenly
dancers gliding by

The Aurora Borealis or Northern Lights is a spectacular natural phenomenon only seen in the far northern hemisphere

The role of the Lord Lieutenant

In November 2002 I was given the great honour by Her Majesty The Queen to be Lord Lieutenant of Banffshire. The Lord Lieutenant is the Queen's representative in Banffshire, and is appointed personally by the Sovereign. It is a great privilege to serve Her Majesty and Banffshire in this way. I am the 11th Lord Lieutenant and first Lady Lord Lieutenant of the county. I am assisted by a Vice Lord Lieutenant and six Deputy Lieutenants.

My duties include:

- Organising visits to the county by members of the Royal Family
- Co-ordinating nominations to the Royal Garden Parties. Nominations are provided by the Deputy Lieutenants of Banffshire and by the local councils, and cover people from all walks of life, particularly those who carry out public or voluntary work
- The presentation of medals and awards on behalf of Her Majesty
- Arranging for representatives to be present at War Memorials on Remembrance Sunday
- Delivering Her Majesty The Queen's messages of congratulations on Diamond Weddings and 100th Birthdays
- Liaison with the Army, Royal Navy, Air Force, TA, local Cadet Force and British Legion
- Involvement in many charity organisations

1   *C Company, 2nd Battalion, The Highlanders Army Cadet Force*

2   *Lucy McPhee – Lord Lieutenant's Cadet*

3   *HRH The Princess Royal at the Boyndie Centre*

4   *HRH The Duke of Rothesay at Keith*

5   *HRH The Duke of York at Drumin Castle*

6   *HRH The Princess Royal at the Boyndie Centre*

7   *HRH The Duke of York at the Glenfiddich Distillery*

8   *HRH The Duke of Rothesay at Speyside Home*

9   *HRH The Duke of York with C Company, 2nd Battalion, The Highlanders Army Cadet Force*

10   *HRH The Earl of Wessex at Buckie*

11   *TRHs The Duke and Duchess of Rothesay at Walkers of Aberlour*

12   *Veterans' Day flypast, 2008*

Toast to Banff

The 'Toast to the County of Banff' by my predecessor at a very difficult time when local authority boundaries were being re-organised, provides a perfect way to conclude this photographic journey through our beloved county.

By Provost J.A.S. McPherson, M.A., LL.B., County Convener, at the Luncheon following the final Meeting of Banff County Council on Friday 9th May 1975.

As Tennyson wrote in *Morte d'Arthur*, "The old order changeth yielding place to the new and God fulfils himself in many ways lest one good custom should corrupt the world".

Banffshire has a long and proud history and those of us who belong to or live in the County cannot be blamed if we view with some disfavour and apprehension the changes which now prejudice its continuing identity.

If one looks at a map, Banffshire appears like a wedge pushed in from the rocky shores of the Moray Firth stretching some 30 miles from the Tore of Troup in the east to the Burn of Tynet in the west, and penetrating a distance of some 50 miles deep into the high wind-swept plateau of the Cairngorms. As a result it offers a considerable diversity of topography which is one of its most interesting and attractive features. Indeed, I would suggest to you that if you were to look for a rich and balanced environment in which a man could live and make a career and have for himself and his family a full life,

you would have to look far before you found anywhere that met these requirements so well as the County of Banff.

Here there has grown up over the years a renowned and skilled agriculture benefiting from the resourcefulness of the early pioneers but taking full advantage of improved methods and scientific research – an agriculture from which other agricultures have been ready to borrow in stock and in wisdom.

The rugged coastline has seen the growth of small communities picking, in earlier years, a very meagre living from the inshore fishing grounds. It is to these intrepid and industrious pioneers that the coastal burghs and villages of today owe their origin, and from these modest beginnings a great new fishing industry has grown, taking advantage of science and technology and bringing prosperity to the County. With the natural resources developed in this way, there have grown in turn the industries based upon them and they are still growing directly out of these great traditions of soil and shore.

Then through a God-given blessing of ingenuity and inspiration emerged the whisky industry, the greatest trouble-free money spinner the British Treasury has ever enjoyed, and of course in Banffshire we must not forget the development

of a thriving tourist industry whose potential has not yet been fully exploited.

Above all, in Banffshire we enjoy a way of life with great richness of local dialect, culture and art, and a genuine friendly and open-hearted environment ever ready to welcome strangers and new ideas.

But at the risk of being criticised as a sentimentalist, I would suggest that to Banffshire folk, to you and to me, and perhaps particularly to those born and brought up in the County who are now living abroad or in other parts of the United Kingdom, Banffshire means much more than those things of which I have spoken. Banffshire is many things – a past, a present and a future – a small friendly County of under 45 thousand people, and yet a County with a great tradition and a fine heritage.

She is the ghosts of the men and women who have made her great – her churchmen and her scholars, her farmers and her fishermen, her tradesmen and her administrators, her craftsmen and those in the professions.

She is beauty – the rugged grandeur of the snow-capped Cairngorms; the sunset over the Moray Firth on a late summer evening.

She is her rich heritage of old castles and buildings; of historical and architectural interest; Auchindown and Boyne, Inchdrewer and Findlater, Balvenie and Drumin.

She is a County of small Burghs, the Royal Burghs of Banff and Cullen and the Burghs of Aberchirder and Aberlour, Buckie and Dufftown, Findochty and Keith, Macduff, Portknockie and Portsoy, each with its own identity and strong sense of community. She is the small villages and communities from Crovie to Newmill, from Sandend to Craigellachie, from Fordyce to Portgordon, from Whitehills to Tomintoul, from Gardenstown to Cornhill.

She is her many fine schools both past and present, and the rich legacy of educational achievement and attainment which was for many years the envy of other parts of the country.

She is the golden sands at Banff Links, Sandend and Cullen, the bustle of the fish markets at Buckie, Whitehills and Macduff, the distilleries on the whisky trail from Inverboyndie to Glenlivet, from Inchgower to Glenfarclas, from Glenglassaugh to Glenfiddich.

She is her rich farmlands, her extensive woodlands, the vast heather moorlands of the alpine plateau, the land of the ptarmigan, the white hare, the lordly buck and the golden eagle.

She is her fighting men at Mons and Gallipoli, Alamein and Anzio, Korea and Aden – the Gordons, Black Watch and Argylls, the Royal Navy, the Royal Air Force, the men whose names grace the granite memorials in every town and village throughout the County.

She is the intriguing changes of local dialect as one moves from east to west or from the coast to the upper reaches of the County. She is the lilt of her songs. She is the warm-hearted friendliness and hospitality of her people, ever-ready to welcome the stranger and make him feel at home. She is the handclasp of Auld Lang Syne at Hogmanay as the bells ring in each New Year.

Banffshire is all these things, and more, in one small friendly County, a pulsating force that fuses them all together as her story sweeps through the centuries, and because of her there should be pride in the hearts of each one of us here this afternoon.

Changes stemming from the reorganisations of local government are inevitable, and as to the future of the County one can but hazard a guess. But two forecasts I would make with a hope and conviction drawn from the inspiration of the past: one – the people of Banffshire will stoutly re-affirm their determination to retain the County's identity, and two – the County, despite the changes which threaten its continued existence, will survive and flourish.

I trust that you will pledge with me your determination to do all you can to ensure that these two forecasts are realised as I ask you to charge your glasses and rise to toast with me the County of Banff.

(signature)

Auld Lang Syne

by Robert Burns in 1788

Should auld acquaintance be forgot,
and never brought to mind?
Should auld acquaintance be forgot,
and auld lang syne?

For auld lang syne, my dear,
for auld lang syne,
we'll tak a cup o' kindness yet,
for auld lang syne.
And surely ye'll be your pint-stoup!
And surely I'll be mine!
And we'll tak a cup o' kindness yet,
for auld lang syne.

We twa hae run about the braes,
and pou'd the gowans fine;
But we've wander'd mony a weary fit,
sin' auld lang syne.

We twa hae paidl'd in the burn,
frae morning sun till dine;
But seas between us braid hae roar'd
sin' auld lang syne.

And there's a hand, my trusty fiere!
And gives a hand o' thine!
And we'll tak a right guid willie-waught,
for auld lang syne.

First published in 2009 by Heritage House Group, Norfolk NR18 9RS.
Telephone 01603 813319
www.hhgroup.co.uk

Designed by Nick McCann
Produced by Heritage House Group.

Pink - ISBN 978-0-85101-432-6
Blue - ISBN 978-0-85101-436-4

Printed in China   E-81544-1/09

For the people of Banffshire – by the people of Banffshire